DRAMA
5-14

A PRACTICAL APPROACH
TO CLASSROOM DRAMA

IRENÉ RANKIN

Hodder & Stoughton

A MEMBER OF THE HODDER HEADLINE GROUP

Order queries: please contact Bookpoint Ltd, 39 Milton Park, Abingdon, Oxon OX14 4TD. Telephone: (44) 01235 400414, Fax: (44) 01235 400454. Lines are open from 9.00–6.00, Monday to Saturday, with a 24 hour message answering service. Email address: orders@bookpoint.co.uk

British Library Cataloguing in Publication data
A catalogue record for this title is available from The British Library

ISBN 0 340 65562 3

First published 1995
Impression number   15   14   13   12   11   10   9   8   7
Year   2003   2002   2001   2000   1999   1998

Designed and typeset by Artisan Graphics, Edinburgh.
Printed in Great Britain for Hodder & Stoughton Educational, a division of Hodder Headline Plc, 338 Euston Road, London NW1 3BH by Hobbs the Printers Ltd, Totton, Hampshire SO40 3WX

Material presented in boxes like this may be photocopied for use in the school or institution only.

CONTENTS

Acknowledgements

I wish to record my appreciation of the inspiration given to me over the years by students and teachers, especially those encountered during my years at St Andrew's College, Glasgow. My thanks are also due to the staff of Netherlee Primary School, Glasgow, for guidance on what teachers may need in a book of this kind, and finally to Robin, who rescued me when the computer 'beat' me, and who also introduced me to the joys of desktop publishing!

For permission to reprint copyright material the author and publisher gratefully acknowledge the following: the Editor of *The Scots Magazine* and Mr Tom Weir for the use of extracts from 'My Month'; the Editor, *Yachting Monthly*, for the extract from Wallace Clark's article, 'An Isle beyond an Isle'; Pan Books Ltd, for the two extracts from *The Diary of Anne Frank* by Anne Frank; Dumfries and Galloway Regional Council, Education Department, for the use of previously published material in the Staff Development Package, *Drama in Education*; and Mr Jack Ducat, for his letter to *The Scots Magazine*.

Every effort has been made to secure permission for material which is under copyright; the author and publisher apologise for any error or omission in the above and will take note of any additional information supplied to them.

Preface

I do and I understand
(Chinese Proverb)

I know I'm lucky. I chose to be a drama teacher. Mind you, back in the 60s, newly qualified, I wasn't too sure of exactly what I was meant to be doing! Drama was about the development of the whole person; an ambitious aim, which a young inexperienced teacher had difficulty in explaining to colleagues who expected her to be dealing with speech problems or 'getting them to speak properly'.

I first realised that I might have the makings of a useful teacher in my first year of teaching. In those days, role play wasn't called by that name – in Brian Way's *Development Through Drama* (Longman, 1967), it is described as 'social drama'. But, by whatever name, the technique proved invaluable to one of my pupils.

'Oh, Miss! It was great! They asked all the questions we did [acted-out] in class, and I've got the job!'

'Oh! That's marvellous! And what's the job?'

'I pick bits of fluff off the new carpets as they roll by. And there's music playing all the time!'

A small, yet notable and gratifying triumph. Through role play, the pupil's self esteem had risen and she had confidence for the interview.

From then on, my drama teaching developed as I developed as a teacher; my pupils taught me how to hone and refine my teaching skills, and often gave me further moments of satisfaction. But drama offers more than role play. You can give pupils the opportunity to immerse themselves in an incident; in their imagination they can travel back in time, or assume the identity of a character in a novel, or cross the oceans to faraway places. You can encourage pupils to experience and then reflect upon their involvement with the drama, adding to their knowledge and understanding of other people, times and places. Drama work offers great opportunities for language development, reinforcing speaking and listening skills, all within an accessible and enjoyable framework. Although a drama lesson might concentrate on movement and miming skills, language and communication have vital roles to play too, for the children have to listen, think about and react to the drama. Their involvement in acting-out requires practice in both speaking and listening, while in negotiating and responding to drama, pupils exercise their social skills, adapting their language to the chosen drama situation. In addition, you can use drama within cross-curricular topics, to enhance learning in many subject areas.

This book has been written to help the teacher to satisfy the curriculum needs and guidelines. In the English Curriculum for England and Wales, Drama comes within AT1, Speaking and Listening. In Scotland, Drama is one of a group of subjects labelled Expressive Arts.

England & Wales **National Curriculum Drama** (included in the National Curriculum Order for English)	Scotland **National Guidelines – Expressive Arts 5–14**	
ATTAINMENT TARGETS	OUTCOME/ATTAINMENT (not listed in order of importance)	DRAMA STRANDS
AT1 Speaking and listening	**Using** materials, techniques, skills and media	Investigating and experimenting Using movement and mime Using language
	Expressing feelings, ideas, thoughts and solutions	Creating and designing Communicating and presenting
	Evaluating and **appreciating**	Observing, listening, reflecting, describing and responding
End of Key Stage Statements Key Stages 1(7 years) levels 1–3 2 (11 years) levels 2–5 3 (14 years) levels 3–7		Attainment Targets Levels A–E (5–14 years) (Age description is not appropriate)

The differences in the Scottish Guidelines means that the levels therein are not confined to any specific age or year group as the Expressive Arts 5–14 document makes clear: 'What is learned and taught will be much more than the sum of the target descriptors' (page 9). Thus a child with learning difficulties aged 8 could still be working towards level A or B. A gifted child aged 8 might be working towards level D.

INTRODUCTION

When I worked with both students and teachers who saw the value of drama, it always concerned me that I often heard 'But it'll work for you. You are the drama expert!' What use was it, if after an in-service session or demonstration lesson, the non-specialists felt inadequate on their own? This book has been written for these non-specialists, who can see the value of teaching drama techniques, but who need more help and confidence when it comes to planning and teaching lessons.

I wanted to write material which would stand on its own, be easy to read and understand, and most important of all, be practical and usable in the classroom. I started to analyse my lessons. They followed the same pattern.

1. A strong beginning to grasp the attention and attract commitment to the task;
2. A line of development, using questioning and answering techniques;
3. Reflection on what had happened during the session.

The next stage was to devise the three-column structure, derived from my work as a cross-curricular tutor.

Lesson Outline

This is the column which should be read or written first. It details the content from beginning to end, but at times gives options, as you will have to react to the class, depending on their needs.

Teacher Role

This is your help-line column! Here suggestions are given on controlling the acting-out, and how you can also actively participate within the drama.

Pupil Activity

In this column are notes about what you would expect the class to be doing; but remember, all classes are different and you must be prepared to deal with unexpected reactions!

Lesson plans

This book is not a scripted play. The lessons should not be followed rigidly, line by line as set out here – they are my guidelines. **You** must decide where your emphasis will lie in each case, according to the particular needs of the class. Do not be afraid to repeat lessons. Reinforcement is as important in Drama as in other subjects, and lessons can be repeated with children taking different roles and offering more ideas, taking the drama further because they have had time to reflect on the previous lesson.

Each lesson begins with a page which lists the aims and the resources required, and outlines the organisation of the lesson. The latter prepares you for the type of drama teaching which will be involved. The lesson might begin with a whole group exercise, and then break down into smaller groups, finishing with a group discussion. Details are also shown of how the content of the lesson relates to the Level descriptions of the National Curriculum for England and Wales and the Outcomes and Strands of the Scottish Curriculum.

The above may seem to be a rather tight structure, but once a teacher has the confidence to allow the participants to make decisions and to move the drama forward, then that structure can become less formal. I have found that teachers have been able to follow this format and use it successfully. Teachers adapt the material, to the extent that I would not recognise it as having been written by me, and that is great! They are making the ideas their own, to suit their children.

This book is your introduction to a structured approach, an approach which will still allow **you** to be in control, and to enjoy the response you have from your pupils.

Topics The following is a list of topics in this book with suggestions for cross-curricular work.

1 LAND OF STORY BOOK – Key Stage 1 and Levels A/B
Two well-known stories are looked at in an unusual way, stressing the children's own contributions. 'The Sad Giant' gives pupils an opportunity to take responsible roles, in a highly controlled way.

National Curriculum	National Guidelines
English: *Speaking and Listening*	English Language: *Talking about experiences, feelings and opinions.*
Mathematics: *Shape, Position and Measures*	Mathematics: *Shape, Space and Movement*

2 KATY MORAG AND THE TWO GRANDMOTHERS
– Key Stage 2 and Level B
Using Mairi Hedderwick's book about a little girl and her town grannie's visit to a Scottish island, these lessons enable pupils to explore differing lifestyles.

National Curriculum	National Guidelines
Geography: *Settlement*	Environmental Studies Social Subjects: *Understanding People and Place*
Music: *Performing and Composing*	Music: *Communicating and Presenting*

3 THE SIX LIVES OF FANKLE THE CAT by George Mackay Brown
– Key Stage 2 and Level C
These two lessons show the cross-curricular possibilities of studying a novel. In this case, George Mackay Brown's novel is the starting point of each lesson. 'Pirates' involves the class in a fantasy journey; in 'Egyptians' the pupils are 'expert' archeologists journeying back in time.

National Curriculum	National Guidelines
English: *Speaking and Listening*	English Language: *Talking in groups*
History: *Unit 6 Ancient Egypt*	Environmental Studies Social Subjects: *Understanding People in the Past*

4 FLANNAN ISLE – Key Stage 2 and Level D
This poem, by WW Gibson, is the starting-point for the class to attempt to solve the mystery surrounding the disappearance of lighthouse keepers in 1900.
The different styles of the three lessons use various drama strategies.

National Curriculum	National Guidelines
English: *Speaking and Listening Reading*	English Language: *Talking about texts*
History: *Victorian Britain*	English Language: *Audience awareness*

5 THE DESPERATE JOURNEY – Key Stage 2/3 and Levels C/D
This novel by Kathleen Fidler is an exciting story about a family, and it deals with several issues in ways which will capture the interest of children, no matter where they may live. The social effects of the Highland Clearances, of the Industrial Revolution and finally of emigration to a strange country, are all dealt with during the course of the novel.

National Curriculum	**National Guidelines**
History: *Study Unit 3a*	Environmental Studies
	Social Subjects: *Understanding People in the Past*
Physical Education: *Dance*	Physical Education: *Creating and Designing*
English: *Speaking and Listening*	English Language: *Talking in groups*

6 CHILDREN IN WAR – Key Stages 2/3 and Levels D/E
The three lessons describe life for children during the Second World War. They enable pupils to understand the sufferings of children like themselves, not only in the past but in present-day conflicts around the world.

National Curriculum	**National Guidelines**
History: *Study Unit 3b* *Britons at War*	Environmental Studies
	Social Subjects: *Understanding People in the Past*

7 THE SEA
The three lessons in this topic demonstrate how a single theme can be used with different age groups.

1. 'Trip to the Seaside' – Key Stage 1 and Levels A/B

National Curriculum	**National Guidelines**
Geography: *Places*	Science: *Understanding Earth and Space*

2. 'The Seal People' – Key Stage 2 and Level C

National Curriculum	**National Guidelines**
English: *Speaking and Listening*	English Language: *Listening in order to respond to texts*

3. 'The Bridge Question' – Key Stages 2/3 and Levels D/E

National Curriculum	**National Guidelines**
Geography: *Settlement 9b*	Religious and Moral Education: *Personal Search*

8 PERSEUS AND THE GORGON'S HEAD – Key Stage 2 and Levels C/D
These lessons were devised for a class of boys who were to present their drama work at the end of term, but their teacher wished classroom drama to be the starting point. This could not work without an integrated arts approach and a recognition of the fables of Ancient Greece!

National Curriculum	**National Guidelines**
Art, Music, Physical Education	All Expressive Arts!
History: *Study Unit 4* *Ancient Greeks, Myths and Legends*	

Glossary ***'I can't understand the jargon!'***
(perplexed teacher)

Every subject has its own jargon, and here follows a short glossary of drama terms:

ACTING OUT — 'The distinctive feature of Drama' (*Learning Through Drama* McGregor et al, Heinemann 1977): the process of projection into imagined or assumed roles or situations, ie, whenever a child takes on any role in any drama situation, he or she is 'acting out'.

Acting out includes all of the following:

1. Adopting a role – exploring a situation as an imagined character. This leads to
2. Characterisation – the investigation and portrayal in depth of a specific role.
3. Improvisation – unscripted drama work.
4. Mime used to be described as the use of movement (sometimes with masks) to communicate meaning or narrative without words. But modern mime artists often use sound and the spoken word to augment the mimed action. This works well with children.
5. Role play – an activity in which participants (usually in pairs or a small group), investigate a real life or imaginary situation, either as self or as another person. This can lead to
6. Simulation – the recreation of an event or situation authentically constructed in order to gain insight and depth.
7. Dance drama – a story or situation explored and conveyed through a sequence of rhythmic creative movement, usually accompanied by sound, percussion or music.
8. Script work – working from a script or moving towards the creation of a script. (The lessons which follow do not use scripts, and in the topic where presentation is discussed, 'Perseus and the Gorgon's Head', the spoken words should come from the improvisations.)

To complete the learning process, within and at the completion of acting out, the following takes place:

Reflection – here the teacher, by various means, can test out what learning has occurred.

Evaluation – the children respond to the experience, commenting, where appropriate, on their own and others' contributions.

The acting-out process develops:

1. Concentration – being able to devote complete attention to the drama.
2. Visualisation – being able to recall, in the mind's eye, recognised places and situations.
3. Imagination – being able to project into an unknown situation.
4. Trust – being able to feel confident with the peer group and the teacher.
5. Language skills.

TEACHER IN ROLE or TIR — The teacher assumes a role within the drama, becoming a part of it. Depending on the type of role, the children can be led, influenced, challenged, asked for help or left on their own.

TENSION — A point in the drama where something unusual or unexpected happens. The drama is driven forwards by either challenging the pupils or asking them to solve a problem. Sometimes the tension might occur as a change of atmosphere is introduced with music or a change in the lighting. A session with no tension of any kind is probably not a drama lesson but a movement lesson or drama exercise!

The teacher should use

SPACE — Choose the appropriate space to suit the drama, for example:
Classroom where children can feel secure,
Hall when movement or journeys are required,
Use of levels where change of location or a feeling of authority is required.

CONTROL — Devices which are built into drama situations in order that the activity can proceed and develop in a satisfactory and creative way. These include:
the *drama contract* (the class formally agree to abide by the rules of the drama)
a *tambour* (the sound meaning to STOP and FREEZE);
the use of *routine*
making the drama *interesting and worthwhile*.

The children should show

COMMITMENT — A belief in the drama.

INTERACTION — The ability to respond to others.

LEARNING — Insight and understanding of the teacher's chosen aims.

SATISFACTION — The 'good feeling' of a task well done.

LAND OF STORY BOOK

Introduction These three lessons need not be part of a topic, but could be used as an introduction to the drama way of working for young children. The methods can be applied to similar stories or rhymes.

The first lesson, 'Little Red Riding Hood' can introduce a class of children who have never done drama to a highly controlled situation, initially sitting in a circle, where they talk about Red Riding Hood's basket and what it might contain. They then go on to act out the characters, controlled by suitable percussion for each.

'The Three Bears' is *not* an enactment of the story, which the children should know in advance. It is an opportunity to introduce occupational mime, linked to the beginning of character work. Here we are making the fairy-story characters more like humans, not just cardboard cut-outs. There is also a move away from the stereotyped role.

The final lesson in this section is not a well known story, and is acted out as it is being told. In 'The Sad Giant who had no Friends' the children are asked to concentrate, listen and respond to the Teacher in Role (TIR). They will also be asked to make suggestions and contributions as the lesson progresses, so that they are involved in the process of the composition of the story.

Lesson title

Little Red Riding Hood

	OUTCOME/ ATTAINMENT TARGET	STRANDS
Levels: A/B **Key Stage 1** Levels **1–2**	**Using** *materials, techniques, skills and media*	Investigating and experimenting: **explore simple movement and mime**
Date:		Using movement and mime: **respond to teacher's voice and musical instruments**
Learning Aims: 1 **Listen and respond** 2 **Enjoy bringing a well-known story to life**		Using language: **use language appropriately**
Other Information **This lesson uses sound to help movement in character**	**Expressing** *feelings, ideas, thoughts and solutions*	Creating and designing: **decide on gifts for Grannie — sustain the role of wolf**
Resources: **Tambour Cymbals Maracas**		Communicating and presenting: **communicate ideas in the whole class group**
Organisation 1 **Circle** 2 **Whole group acting out**	**Evaluating** and **Appreciating**	Observing, listening, reflecting, describing and responding: **participate fully in all the activities, showing concentration and commitment**

Lesson Outline	Teacher Role	Pupil Activity
Introduction		
Let's all sit in a circle.	Organises.	
Would you like to do the story of Little Red Riding Hood today?	Sets up contract.	Agree to participate.
Let's draw the *shape* of Red Riding Hood's basket in front of us...	Cross-curricular link.	Visualisation.
Today I'll have a *round* basket.		
What shape is yours —, and yours — etc. (three pupils).		Decision-making.
Now, what will we put in our basket to take to Grannie?	Questions.	Decision-making.
Accept suggestions.	(NB If flowers are suggested, say we will pick them on the way through the woods.)	
Items like apples or small cakes should be mimed and counted into the basket.	Cross-curricular link and visualisation.	All participate with language and mime.
Put three different items into the basket, eg six apples; one chocolate cake; two pots of jam (which kind?).		Mime.
Good!	Encourages.	
Development		
Now, put on your red cloak.	Directs.	
Let's skip off into the woods.	*Skipping rhythm on the tambour.*	Rise and move.
Look, here are some lovely flowers. Let's pick them for Grannie.		Act out.
It's a hot day and Grannie always goes for a sleep after dinner... and here is a grassy bank.		Listen.
Let's lie down and have a little sleep.		Lie down.
Now...	Introduces *tension.*	
Not far away in a cave, the *Wolf* lies sleeping.		
	Sounds cymbal.	

Lesson Outline	Teacher Role	Pupil Activity
When I sound the cymbal again, you *will become the Wolf lying sleeping in the cave.*		New role adopted *while lying down.*
Now, you are the Wolf.		
Wake up and sniff. You smell – a little girl.	*Sounds cymbal.*	Act out.
With your nose close to the ground – follow the scent.	*Sounds cymbal.*	
Lift your nose higher – and higher – until you are walking on your hind legs.	(NB Always have animals walking on hind legs — Disney style! Good for creating animal movement.)	
Follow the smell, then peer round a tree and see...	*Sounds cymbal.*	Acting out continued.
Little Red Riding Hood.		
Ooooh!		
'I know where she's going! She's going to Grannie's cottage.'	In role as Wolf.	
Rub your front paws together.		Continue being the Wolf.
'I know a quick way. I'll get there before her.' And quickly off you trot... until you get to Grannie's cottage.	Wolf voice again.	
Knock on the door.	*Knocks with tambour.*	
Grannie says, 'Who is it?'	Grannie voice.	
'Little Red Riding Hood.'	Uses appropriate voices throughout.	
'Come in.'		
And as soon as she sees the Wolf, Grannie starts to shake all over.		
Be Grannie.	*Sounds maracas.*	Change role quickly in response to sound.
And she runs and hides in the wardrobe.	*Sounds cymbal.*	
You are the Wolf again.		Become the Wolf.
Pick up Grannie's night cap and put it on. Climb into bed –and pull the sheets up to your chin – and wait...		Act out.

Lesson Outline	Teacher Role	Pupil Activity
	Sounds cymbal.	
Now *I'll* be Little Red Riding Hood.	Goes into role.	React to TIR.
I skip through the wood.	*Sounds tambour.*	
I knock on the door.		
The Wolf says '...	*Sounds tambour.*	
I open the door and go in.	*Sounds cymbal as cue.*	Vocal participation.
'Oh! Grannie! What big *eyes* you have!'		
(Wait for vocal response and react to it.)	*Sounds cymbal.*	Vocal participation.
'Oh! Grannie! What big *ears* you have.'		
	Sounds cymbal. NB Be near the tambour ready to sound!	Vocal participation.
'Oh! Grannie! What big *teeth* you have!'		Vocal participation plus probably simultaneous lunge.
	Freeze signal. (NB You *must* be close to the tambour – the cymbal will probably not be needed! The children are ready to *get* you! As soon as they move – shout *freeze* and sound the tambour loudly!)	
(Speaking quickly:) Not far away a wood-cutter is cutting down trees. *Be the wood-cutter.*	*Tambour.*	Change role.
He hears Little Red Riding Hood calling, 'Help!' He runs up the path and *kills the Wolf dead.*	*Tambour.*	Act out.
But who is still in the wardrobe?		
	Maracas. Let the children adopt a role without any organisation.	Recall. They can *be* Grannie or help her.
Help Grannie into her bed.		
What might make her feel better? Have we anything we can give her?	Questions.	Problem-solving.
Reflection and Evaluation	Leads discussion about what they have been doing. Would they like to do the lesson once more?	

Land of Story Book

Lesson title **The Three Bears**

OUTCOME/ ATTAINMENT TARGET	STRANDS
Using materials, techniques, skills and media	Investigating and experimenting: **explore simple movement and make decisions** Using movement and mime: **use mime and gesture appropriate to the role** Using language: **use language appropriate to the role**
Expressing feelings, ideas, thoughts and solutions	Creating and designing: **develop a role, with support, and start to improvise in a group** Communicating and presenting: **share the outcome of their work with the class** (NB if they wish!)
Evaluating and **Appreciating**	Observing, listening, reflecting, describing and responding: **discuss the characters, relate their activities to their own lifestyle, listen and watch others working**

Levels: **A/B**   Key Stage **1**
                   Levels **1–3**

Date:

Learning Aims:
1 **Practise mime skills**
2 **Make decisions**

Other Information
This lesson encourages the children to think of everyday actions for fairy-tale characters

Resources:
    None

Organisation
1 **Miming in a circle, led by the teacher**
2 **Working together, but in groups of three**

Lesson Outline	Teacher Role	Pupil Activity
Introduction		
Sit in a circle.	Organises space.	Prepare to listen.
Can you remember the story of 'The Three Bears'?	Introduces the context.	Respond.
Who is in the story?	Questions.	Respond.
Would you like to find out more about the Three Bears?	Introduces new but related context.	Express interest.
Development		
Well...		
Let's all be Daddy Bear first of all.	Introduces the role.	Think about being Daddy Bear.
I'll let you into a secret.	Whispers.	Listen.
He loves to keep fit.		
All stand up.	Uses lively speech.	Stand, ready to work.
Feel your strong muscles.	Moves around the circle, expressing astonishment with the size of their muscles!	Act out.
Look at your strong arms and your strong legs...!		
Now, every morning, Daddy Bear opens the window and breathes in the fresh air.		Listen.
I wonder if your window opens by pulling it up, or pushing it out...?	Queries, but does not ask any one child.	
Mine goes upwards.	Mimes.	
Open *your* windows.	Directs.	Mime.
Breathe *in* and *out*, *in* and *out*.	Directs.	Act out.
Now for your exercises...		
Run on the spot...	Leads the action.	Follow the teacher's lead if necessary.
Touch you toes...		
Now get dressed...		
It's a lovely morning.	Controls by slowing the lesson down.	Listen.
Off you go into the garden.		

Lesson Outline	Teacher Role	Pupil Activity
Open the garden shed... Take out a spade.	Leads the action.	Mime.
The garden needs a bit of digging before you plant the vegetables.		
So let's dig in this garden...	Leads the miming.	Mime.
Here comes the paper-boy...		
Good morning, Mr Bear!	Into role (TIR) as paper-boy.	
Here's your morning paper.		Catch thrown paper.
Sit down in the garden to read the paper.	Directs out of role.	Follow direction.
Now be Mrs Bear!	Directs.	Change roles.
Mrs. Bear goes to Weightwatchers.	Describes the character and then leads a repeat of the previous exercises but slowly and with humour.	Act out.
She does her exercises *very slowly*....		
Then she sets the table.		
What does she need on the table?	Queries and takes their suggestions, miming the actions.	Respond and mime the setting of the table.
Now remember to stir the porridge... And take a little taste...	Leads the action.	Mime.
Freeze.	Controls.	
Baby Bear loves his bed, and never wants to get up in the morning.	Describes.	Listen.
Curl up in bed.	Directs and uses Mummy Bear voice.	Act out.
You hear Mummy Bear calling you:		
"Wake up, Baby Bear!"		
But you curl up tighter!		
"Wake up, Baby Bear!"		
You snuggle down deeper and turn over...		
Now, there is one thing that Baby Bear likes better than his bed, and that is – his *food!*	Gives further background.	Listen.

Lesson Outline	Teacher Role	Pupil Activity
"Get up, Baby Bear, or you won't get any breakfast!"	TIR as Mummy Bear.	Respond appropriately.
So quickly get dressed and come to breakfast.	Directs.	Act out.
All sit down.	Controls and directs.	Come out of role.
Now, listen and remember who you are.	Numbers them off in threes, calling them by the character's name. Daddy Bear... Mummy Bear... Baby Bear. If there is an extra person, the last group has twin bears. (NB Pay no attention to the sex of the children - quickly tell them their roles.)	Listen to their role name.
Daddy Bears – stand up.		One third of the class act out while the others watch.
What do you do first thing in the morning?	Leads Daddy Bears through the morning activities, keep-fit, digging, etc.	
Sit down and read the paper – but you can watch what is happening to the rest of the family.		
Mummy Bears – stand up and let's do your exercises.	As before leads the Mummy Bears through *their* activities.	
Now set the table...		
And stir the porridge...		
Baby Bears, curl up in bed.	Leads the two groups.	Groups act out.
Mummy Bears call up to them:		
One, two, three, get up, Baby Bear.		
And again.		
Mummy Bear, off you go and tell Daddy Bear what is the matter.	Encourages interaction using children's own words. (THIS COULD BE AN ASSESSMENT POINT.)	Two groups interact.
Up you both go to Baby Bear.	Builds in a control, but still must keep a careful eye on the class!	All groups, working in threes, act out.
Without touching him, find a way to get him up!		
Freeze.	Controls.	Responds to the control signal.

Lesson Outline	Teacher Role	Pupil Activity
Sit down.	Settles the class down.	Sit.
Who managed to get Baby Bear up?	Asks them to report on what happened.	Talk about their work.
How did you do it?		
Would you like to do this story again?		
Let's change it a bit.	Suggests a slight difference.	
Today is the day Mummy Bear goes out to work as a... (eg Lollipop Lady).	Asks what job she might do.	Suggest a job.
Who will make breakfast today?	Will they suggest Daddy Bear?	
This time, Mummy Bears get up first and do their exercises.	Leads Mummy Bears through the actions appropriate to her chosen job.	Mummy Bears act out.
Pick up your lollipop, (or whatever is appropriate) and go off to school.		
Stop the traffic to let the children across.	(Suit the actions to whatever is Mummy Bear's chosen occupation!)	
Now you can sit on the wall and wait for the latecomers.		
Daddy Bears, exercise time again!	Leads Daddy Bears through their actions.	Daddy Bears act out.
Now set the table.		
And stir the porridge.		
What about calling on Baby Bear to get up?		
Still in bed!		
Here is Mummy Bear home from work.	Brings all three together again.	Prepare to work in threes.
Again, *without touching him,* do your best to get Baby Bear up.	Once more watches and controls the groups.	Act out.
Freeze.		
All sit down.	Controls and settles them down.	Sit to listen and participate in the discussion.
Who was successful this time?	Leads discussion.	Are stimulated by the action to participate in the discussion and offer opinions.

Lesson Outline	Teacher Role	Pupil Activity
Reflection and Evaluation What do *you* have for breakfast? Is there anyone in this class like Baby Bear? Does any group want to show us how *they* got Baby Bear up?	Gives opportunity for groups to share their work and introduces them to small-scale presentations. NB *This will not always be appropriate. Decide whether your class is ready.*	If confident, share their work.

Land of Story Book

Lesson title

The Sad Giant who had no Friends

OUTCOME/ ATTAINMENT TARGET	STRANDS

<table>
<tr><td>Levels: A/B   Key Stage 1
Levels 1–3</td></tr>
</table>

Date:

Learning Aims:
1 **Use listening skills**
2 **Respond to Teacher in Role (TIR)**
3 **Assume responsibility**

Other Information
This lesson was devised for a class who needed to practise responding to the Drama Control Signal, and to concentrate on being in role

Resources:
    Control signal –
    Tambour (when struck, the
    class freeze)
    Space in which to move

Organisation
1 **Listening to the story**
2 **Whole class work in role**
3 **Reflection and discussion**

OUTCOME/ ATTAINMENT TARGET	STRANDS
Using materials, techniques, skills and media	Investigating and experimenting: **experimenting with movement; demonstrating inventiveness** Using movement and mime: **using movement and mime with support conveying feelings** Using language: **listening and responding appropriately**
Expressing feelings, ideas, thoughts and solutions	Creating and designing: **exploring a situation with support** Communicating and presenting: **exploring in role, with support**
Evaluating and **Appreciating**	Observing, listening, reflecting, describing and responding: **sustaining interest in the activity; responding and talking about the activity**

Lesson Outline	Teacher Role	Pupil Activity
Introduction		
The class prepare to listen to a story.	Organises the space for listening and acting out.	Settle down.
The Story Begins.	Story teller.	
A Sad Giant lived near a small village. He was a very large Giant. So large that people were really frightened whenever they heard him coming and they ran in the opposite direction. He had no-one to talk to, he had no friends and he was very lonely. The villagers thought they had to keep him happy, so they left out food for him, but of course he had to eat alone, and he wasn't happy at all!		
Development		
Let's all be the villagers!	Encourages the adopting of a role.	Become villagers.
We've got our food ready for the Giant.	TIR as villager.	
I've got bacon for him.		
What have you got?	Queries the group.	Respond appropriately in role.
Where shall we leave it for him?	Queries.	Respond.
Oh! Listen! I hear him coming! Come into my house to hide! We can watch him from behind the curtain.	Controls the action in role.	Keep grouped together beside the leader, (all in role).
Look! He's eating, but very slowly. I wonder why?	Asks rhetorical question – but is prepared to deal with replies.	May hypothesise.
How do you think the Giant is feeling?	Queries.	Think about emotions and communicate their ideas.
Let's try to be the Giant now.	Suggests change of role.	Become giants.
We'll walk quietly so as not to frighten anybody.	Leads movement.	Follow the teacher.
But you don't see anybody.	Continues the action.	
And you have to eat by yourself.	Mimes, in character of Sad Giant.	Use appropriate gesture and facial expression.
Freeze, and become children again.	Controls and directs action.	Come out of role.

Lesson Outline	Teacher Role	Pupil Activity
Come and sit by me, and I'll tell you what happened one day.	Continues the story.	Prepare to listen.
A brother and sister both had birthdays on the same day, and they were the same age. Do you know what people like that are called?	Do they know the word 'twins'?	Respond or otherwise.
Their Mum made them a large birthday cake. What colour might the icing be?	Allows the class to add facts to the story.	Agree on a colour.
What might be put on the cake to decorate it?	As above.	Contribute ideas.
Story continues with acting out simultaneously.		
The children thought the Giant might like a piece of cake.	Story teller.	Listen.
So they crept out of their house and laid pieces of cake on plates on the ground....	While speaking, leads the action.	Listen and carry out the appropriate actions.
Then they sat hidden behind a tree to see what would happen...	As above. (The teacher goes into role and the class watch.) In role as the Giant.	Act out. Sit and watch.
'Oh, what is this? I've never seen this before. I don't think I'll eat this!'	 (Teacher comes out of role.)	
How do you feel when you hear the Giant saying this?	Queries.	Recount feelings.
Do you think you will be brave enough to come out from behind the tree and explain what a birthday cake is?	Challenges.	Respond.
I'll be the Giant again and you will need to explain carefully.	Returns to role.	
(TIR tests out their explanations of birthday cakes.)	In role, responds, questions, sometimes does not understand.	Teach the Giant.
(Finally he dares to take a piece and then enjoys the rest!)	Continues to be persuaded.	Encourage.
'Thank you! Do you think you can persuade everyone else to come and speak to me? I'm so lonely.'	In role, asks the children to perform a task.	Agree.

Lesson Outline	Teacher Role	Pupil Activity
	(Teacher comes out of role.)	
Well, the children know they have nothing to fear from the Giant, but what about the grown ups?	Congratulates them, then suggests new task.	Children will have the responsibility for convincing the adults.
Shall I be one, and you have to persuade me that I needn't be afraid?		All work together until the adult is convinced.
The story continues.	Story teller.	Listen.
The Giant was invited to the birthday party, and from that day to this, he has helped with all the heavy, difficult jobs in the village, and joins in all the fun.		
He was never lonely again.		
Reflection and Evaluation		
Invite comments on the characters in the story.	Leads any discussion... or movement...	Reflect on the experience.
Perhaps become the Giant again, now moving happily.		
	NB Have you learned anything about the class through listening to them during the lesson and the reflection time?	

KATIE MORAG AND THE TWO GRANDMOTHERS

Introduction *Katie Morag and the Two Grandmothers* by Mairi Hedderwick, along with other books in the Katie Morag series, is a popular choice for a Unit Study. It provides an excellent study of contrasts between two people, and in acting out the different lifestyles, the pupils can explore the characters more fully. It is, however, only in the last lesson that there is acting out of what actually happens in the book. As in some of the previous lessons (eg 'The Three Bears'), the characters are used as a starting point for the children to 'flesh them out', and build up clear pictures in their minds what the grandmothers might be like to know, and what happens to them outside the story. This means that Lessons One and Two could also be used to compare people who live on islands and in cities.

These three lessons show a progression in the use of *space*.

In Lesson One, the class can carry out *all* actions at their desks, introducing them to mime and being someone else, or being in role, in a highly controlled situation.

More vigorous movement is required in Lesson Two, but the classroom is still suitable, with desks pushed to one side to allow for lively, yet controlled occupational mime.

The whole class work as a group, and then in pairs in the last lesson, and an empty room, or a sectioned-off part of the hall or gym will give the children room to space out and become involved.

Lesson title

The Lifestyle of Granma Mainland

	OUTCOME/ ATTAINMENT TARGET	STRANDS
Level: B **Key Stage 2** **Levels 3–4**	**Using** materials, techniques, skills and media	Investigating and experimenting: **investigate and suggest Granma Mainland's lifestyle**
		Using movement and mime: **in role as Granma Mainland, use occupational mime**
Date:		Using language: **respond to teacher's questions**
Learning Aims: **1 Expand on the character in the book** **2 Practise occupational mime**		
Resources: **Katie Morag and the Two Grandmothers by Mairi Hedderwick (see Bibliography on page 105)**	**Expressing** feelings, ideas, thoughts and solutions	Creating and designing: **with support, create and adopt the role of Granma Mainland, identifying her characteristics**
		Communicating and presenting: **communicate their ideas to the teacher and the class group**
Organisation **1 Listening to the story** **2 Whole class work in role** **3 Group work – suggested final activity**	**Evaluating** and **Appreciating**	Observing, listening, reflecting, describing and responding: **think about Granma Mainland, and reflect upon what they have decided about her**

21

Lesson Outline	Teacher Role	Pupil Activity
NB This lesson could be taken with all the class at their desks. Space is not essential!		
Introduction		
Read the story up to: 'Och, her and her funny ways!' muttered Grannie Island to herself.	Story teller.	Listen.
Granma Mainland lived a very different kind of life from Grannie Island.	Starts to outline Granma Mainland's lifestyle.	Listen.
She lived in a busy city, in a block of flats.		
So, would she have a garden?	Queries.	Respond.
But she likes flowers - so how could she grow them?	Queries and takes note of the suggestions for future reference.	Offer suggestions.
Development		
Let's look at a day in Granma Mainland's life!	Introduces the context for acting out.	
Into bed...	Directs.	Curl up in their seats.
Does she get up early?	Queries.	Think about her and make presumptions!
When she DOES get up, she takes out her curlers ...	Leads the miming.	All mime the actions.
Puts on her make-up ...		
Gets dressed ...		
Does her hair ...		
Paints her nails ...		
What else might she do?	Queries and leads acting out of reasonable suggestions.	Respond and act out.
Take a little watering can...	N.B. Introduces them *into* the role, without actually telling them they *are* Granma Mainland.	Take on the role without realising it.
Water your window boxes/indoor plants ...		
Put on your outdoor shoes.	Leaves the class to decide on the style of dress.	Make decisions.
I wonder what THEY are like?		
And your hat and coat ...		

Lesson Outline	Teacher Role	Pupil Activity
And off *you* go – down in the lift, and down to the café to have coffee with friends. Now, you're going to buy a new hat for your holiday.	Leads movement.	Move as Granma Mainland.
Try on several hats, looking in the mirror ... Choose the one you like the best ...	Leads the acting out.	Mime.
Now you are back in the flat and need to get ready for your holiday on the island of Struay. What will you need to pack?	Asks them to think of holiday packing for Granma Mainland, *not* for themselves.	Decide on appropriate things for Granma to take.
Carefully pack your suitcase ...	Leads miming.	Mime.
When I click my fingers you are no longer Granma Mainland, but Primary ——, in —— School!	Controls and brings them out of role.	Come out of role.
Suggested Related and Final Activity In groups, draw the things that Granma will be taking with her to Struay.	Organises new activity.	Recall what has been mimed and negotiate what each will include in the suitcase.

Katie Morag and the Two Grandmothers

The Lifestyle of Grannie Island

		OUTCOME/ ATTAINMENT TARGET	STRANDS
Level: **B**	Key Stage **2** Levels **3–4**	**Using** materials, techniques, skills and media	Investigating and experimenting: **investigate and suggest Grannie Island's lifestyle** Using movement and mime: **in role as Grannie Island, use occupational mime** Using language: **respond to teacher's questions**
Date:			
Learning Aims: 1 **Expand on the character in the book** 2 **Develop occupational mime**			
Resources: **Katie Morag and the Two Grandmothers by Mairi Hedderwick (see Bibliography on page 105) Space made in classroom**		**Expressing** feelings, ideas, thoughts and solutions	Creating and designing: **with support, create and adopt the role of Grannie Island, identifying her characteristics** Communicating and presenting: **communicate their ideas to the teacher and the class group**
Organisation: 1 **Whole class work in role** 2 **Suggested final activity – whole class sing a Scottish song**		**Evaluating** and **Appreciating**	Observing, listening, reflecting, describing and responding: **think about Grannie Island and reflect on the differences between her and Granma Mainland**

Lesson Outline	Teacher Role	Pupil Activity
NB This lesson needs more space to move in than the previous one, but desks pushed back in the classroom should provide enough as the lesson is short, and more time would be spent moving from one room to another!		
Introduction		
We've looked at the way Granma Mainland lives. Grannie Island says she has 'fancy ways'. I wonder why?	Leads recall discussion and reflection on Granma Mainland.	Reinforce what they have learned about Granma Mainland.
Let's look at the way *she* lives!	Introduces the context for acting out.	
Development		
Into bed ...	Directs.	Curl up in space.
Does *she* get up early?	Queries.	Think about her and make presumptions!
She puts on her dungarees and her boots.	Leads the miming.	All mime the actions.
What else might she do?		
It's still dark.		
Take a torch and go out to feed the hens ...	Leads the acting out. As before, gradually introduces children into role of Grannie Island.	Act out.
What else might you do?	Queries, accepts reasonable suggestions and leads acting out.	Respond and act out.
The tractor needs oiling.		
Get out the oil can and crawl under the tractor.	Leads acting out.	All mime.
Freeze.	Controls.	Stop and listen.
The shop needs potatoes to sell...	Leads the occupational miming.	Mime as Grannie Island.
so take a spade and dig some potatoes up ...		
and put them in a sack.		
Lift up the sack and put it in the trailer ...		
Climb into the tractor ...		

Lesson Outline	Teacher Role	Pupil Activity
and drive off to the village.		
When I click my fingers you are no longer Grannie Island, but Primary —— in —— School!	Controls and brings them out of role.	Come out of role.
Suggested Final and Related Activity		
Grannie Island likes to sing Scottish songs ...	Organises new activity.	All sing a suitable song.
Gather round and we'll practise one of them.		

Katie Morag and the Two Grandmothers

The Day of the Show

	OUTCOME/ ATTAINMENT TARGET	STRANDS
Level: B **Key Stage 2** **Levels 3–4**	*Using* materials, techniques, skills and media	Investigating and experimenting: **with support, use space imaginatively** Using movement and mime: **participate in a variety of roles, using appropriate gestures, expressions and movement** Using language: **use speech, if they wish, while role-playing**
Date: Learning Aims: 1 **Act out the end of the story, experiencing the feelings of the characters in an 'as if' situation**		
Resources: **Katie Morag and the Two Grandmothers by Mairi Hedderwick (see Bibliography on page 105)** **Space in which to spread out for vigorous and lively movement**	*Expressing* feelings, ideas, thoughts and solutions	Creating and designing: **develop the various roles, at times co-operating with a partner** Communicating and presenting: **work as a group, and in pairs**
Organisation 1 **Whole class in role** 2 **Pair work** 3 **Whole group listen and then discuss**	*Evaluating* and *Appreciating*	Observing, listening, reflecting, describing and responding: **reflect on the relationship between the two Grannies and how it may have changed**

Lesson Outline	Teacher Role	Pupil Activity
NB This lesson *does* need more space to carry out the movements, some of which are large. The reading of the story should be completed before this session.		
Introduction		
Today is the day of the Show.		
First of all we have to raise the tent.		
All together pull on the ropes... One, two, three, PULL One, two, three, PULL.	Leads the class in one big group.	All work together.
Hammer in the pegs.		
Tie up the guy ropes ... lift the tables and chairs into place.	Directs.	Some may work together.
The Lady Artist pulls her goat along the road ...	Leads the class being the Artist.	Mime pulling,
At times it pulls *her* ...		then being pulled.
Polish the silver cups that will be the prizes.	Leads occupational mime.	Mime.
Freeze.	Controls.	Stop and listen.
Development		
Now at Grannie Island's cottage, Grannie and Katie have to try to get the sheep, Alecina, ready for the show! Can you remind me what Alecina had done?	Queries as if he/she has forgotten.	Re-tell that part of the story.
Take a partner.	Helps to organise partners. Directs the pair work, moving around the classroom making comments on their efforts.	Work in pairs, using speech if they wish.
Lift the sheep into the bath.		
Pour in the foam bath...		
Give her a scrub...		
Now lift her out and towel her dry...		
Put in the rollers *very* carefully...		
One of you brush her fleece while the other uses the hair-drier.		

Lesson Outline	Teacher Role	Pupil Activity
What about a little perfume?		
Doesn't she look beautiful? I have never seen such a beautiful sheep! Not only on Struay – but in all Scotland.		
I have pleasure in presenting the silver trophy to you.	TIR as Judge with a large gesture, mimes giving the trophy to all the pairs.	Respond to TIR.
Come and sit down.	Settles the class.	Sit.
Everyone enjoyed the party at Grannie Island's cottage.	Recaps on the end of the story.	Listen.
They all had some soup and the cakes from the bakery stall at the show, and the two Grannies were great friends.		
Reflection and Evaluation		
'And Grannie Island never frowned at Granma Mainland's "fancy ways" ever again. I wonder why?'	Leads discussion.	Reflect on the whole story.

THE SIX LIVES OF FANKLE THE CAT

Introduction   *The Six Lives of Fankle the Cat* by George Mackay Brown tells the story of a cat who comes to live with Jenny, and, through the stories of his lives, reveals his secrets.

The lessons that follow can be used as follow-ups to the chapters on 'The Pirates' or The 'Egyptians', but as they do not actually follow the story-line, they could be used independently or within another topic.

Note   The map on the next page is intended to represent a possible layout of the treasure map – other versions can be drawn, or this one may be photocopied. It includes all the essential details of the drama activity, which are
- a jungle to hack through
- a swiftly flowing river to be crossed without any bridge or stepping stones
- a swamp, complete with alligators
- a treasure in the north-west corner buried under a coconut tree.

Lesson title

The Pirates

	OUTCOME/ ATTAINMENT TARGET	STRANDS
Level: C Key Stage 2 Levels **3–5** Date:	**Using** materials, techniques, skills and media	*Investigating and experimenting:* **use space with ingenuity and imagination to investigate the pirates' world**
Learning Aims: 1 **Enjoy the lively experience** 2 **Practise mime skills** 3 **Co-operate in groups and solve problems**		*Using movement and mime:* **develop occupational mime skills and show inventiveness in use of movement and mime in the journey across the island**
		Using language: **use appropriate 'pirate' language, plan activities and reflect upon them**
Other Information **This lesson can be a follow up to 'King of the Pirates' in The Six Lives of Fankle the Cat by George Mackay Brown, or can be a fantasy lesson on its own.**	**Expressing** feelings, ideas, thoughts and solutions	*Creating and designing:* **develop their roles and respond to TIR**
		Communicating and presenting: **communicate through use of appropriate speech and movement**
Resources: **Space in which to move** **Three treasure maps (one example supplied)**	**Evaluating** and **Appreciating**	*Observing, listening, reflecting, describing and responding:* **reflect upon the drama and also the teacher's role within it**
Organisation 1 **Whole group discussion** 2 **Act out in groups simultaneously** 3 **TIR, as captain, directs whole group work** 4 **Class work in three groups simultaneously** 5 **Reflection and evaluation**		

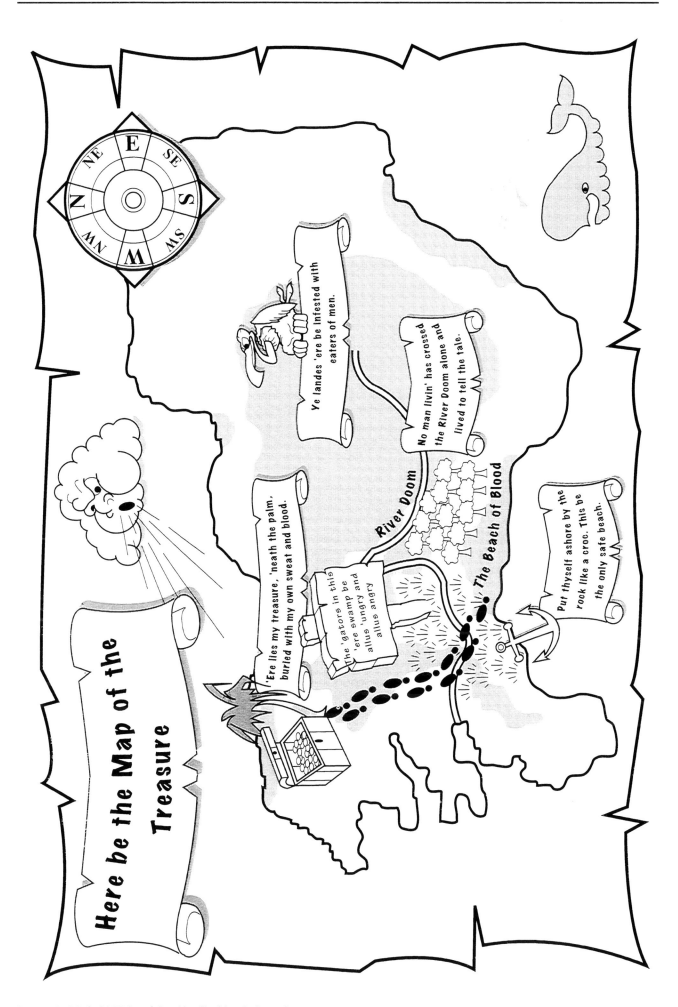

The Beach of Blood

Put thyself ashore by the rock like a croc. This be the only safe beach.

No man livin' has crossed the River Doom alone and lived to tell the tale.

Ye landes 'ere be infested with eaters of men.

'Ere lies my treasure, 'neath the palm, buried with my own sweat and blood.

The 'gators in this 'ere swamp be allus 'ungry and allus angry

River Doom

Here be the Map of the Treasure

Lesson Outline	Teacher Role	Pupil Activity
Introduction		
Today, this room is changing... Changing into a land far away... An island, with palm trees and with warm water all around it. And you will be the people who live on the island. You will not be normal people, but *pirates*, living on your hideaway island.	Introduces the context. Suggests their roles.	Think of the setting.
This is NOT where you've hidden your spare treasure, but where you go to relax.	Supplies more information.	Consider the lifestyle of pirates!
What might Pirates do when they are relaxing?	Queries. Organises groups.	Think of appropriate activities! In groups, sit in space.
In your groups, act out what you do on the island.	Encourages the work, moving around the groups, monitoring and commenting where necessary.	After a *short* discussion, co-operate in their groups.
Development		
Come together, my brave men and women!	TIR as pirate captain.	React to TIR.
Our money is running low. We must sail to our Secret Islands to reclaim our hidden treasure.	Controls in role. Gathers the class to prepare to work as one group.	Gather round the 'Captain'.
We have not sailed for many a year and our ship needs a lot of work done on it.		
Get the paint and brushes ready and paint the ship from bow to stern.	Directs the occupational mime. Explains the nautical terms in role!	Mime.
Look at the rust on these guns. They'll never fire if we need them! Clean and polish them up! And scrub the decks! Load the ship up with boxes of food and barrels of water.	In role, monitors the work. Directs the loading procedures.	Work vigorously. Work together to load the ship.
Now the ship is ready. Pull up the anchor. Hoist the sails.	Directs the actions.	Mime, using language if wished.
Come and sit beside me.	Calms the 'sailors' down after the lively movement.	Sit.
Now I was very careful the last time I was on the Secret Islands.	Promotes interest in the situation.	

Lesson Outline	Teacher Role	Pupil Activity
I made a treasure map which shows the place where the treasure chest is hidden on each island.		
I will divide you into three groups, and you will each go off to a different island to find the treasure.	Organises the groups.	
I shall watch from the ship. The group who are the most careful going and bringing the treasure back, will become my chief officers.	(This could be a means of assessing group co-operation.)	Listen to the task being set.
Here are the maps with the instructions.	Gives out maps and allows time for discussion.	Look at and discuss the problems of the journey.
In your groups, discuss how you might deal with the difficulties on the islands.		
My brave sailors, off you go, and find my treasures!	Starts the acting out.	Work in their groups.
Hide the boat when you land. Hack your way through the jungle. Find a way to cross the swiftly flowing river that has no bridge or stepping stones. Can you cross the swamp which is full of alligators? The treasure is in the north-west corner of the island, under a coconut tree. Carry it back over and through all the obstacles.	TIR 'commands' and monitors the expeditions from a distance. (Try to keep the groups together in time with dealing with a problem. If one gets ahead, they can 'rest', while the others catch up.)	Make decisions and solve the problems encountered on the journey, finally returning to the Captain and the ship.
I'm really pleased with you all – so much so, that since I want to retire, once I've taken *my* share from your treasure chests, each group can use what's left to buy a ship, and you can go into business on your own.	Praises all and brings *this* section to a close.	
	Comes out of role and brings class out of role.	Come out of role.
Reflection and Evaluation		
Who led each group through the obstacles on the island? Were they good at the job? Is this person going to be the Captain? How will you decide? Did I as the Captain lead you? What do you think about that? etc.	Leads discussion, perhaps on leadership skills.	

Lesson title # *The Egyptians*

	OUTCOME/ ATTAINMENT TARGET	STRANDS

Level: **C**	Key Stage **2** Levels **3–5**

Date:

Learning Aims:
1 **Learn about people who lived in Egypt during the 18th dynasty (c1490 BC)**
2 **Develop mime skills**
3 **Co-operate in groups and solve problems**

Other Information
This lesson can be a follow-up to 'Little Thief with the Whiskers that Eats Fish Fins' in Six Lives of Fankle the Cat by George Mackay Brown, or be linked to a topic study on Ancient Egypt.

Resources:
Cymbal
Space in which to move
(If possible use the picture of Tuthmosis from The Search for Ancient Egypt)

Suggested background resources
Pharoahs and Pyramids; The Search for Ancient Egypt; Pharoah's People (see Bibliography on page 105)

Organisation
1 **TIR as archeologist – whole group work**
2 **TIR as Queen Hatshepsut**
3 **Group work – one pupil as Senenmut – mime and movement**
4 **Priest and priestess perform sacred ceremonies**
5 **Group of three – role-play exercise**
6 **Problem-solving followed by acting out**
7 **Reflection**

Using materials, techniques, skills and media

Investigating and experimenting: **investigate the ancient Egyptian world using mime and movement**

Using movement and mime: **use mime and movement in a variety of contexts and roles**

Using language: **use sound and speech in conjunction with movement; plan, and negotiate within drama activities**

Expressing feelings, ideas, thoughts and solutions

Creating and designing: **visualise and create a temple and the ceremonies within it; develop roles and respond to TIR**

Communicating and presenting: **communicate within groups using movement, speech and role play**

Evaluating and **Appreciating**

Observing, listening, reflecting, describing and responding: **participate in discussion reflecting on the drama activities; this may involve wider issues, pulling on experiences from other areas of the curriculum**

Lesson Outline	Teacher Role	Pupil Activity
Introduction Today in our drama we are going to be in the land of Egypt. When I click my fingers we will all become archeologists and we are working in the temple of Deir-el-Bahari.	Outlines the context and the roles. Clicks to denote the start of the drama.	Prepare to work.
Development Come over here, everyone!	In role as Chief Archeologist, organises the group to work in one large group.	In role, respond to the TIR.
Unpack your brushes from your bags and start to carefully brush away the dust from objects.	Directs the mime.	Mime, using careful movements.
I am carefully cleaning the painted wall showing Tuthmosis III offering a sacrifice to his God. (Here in a book is a drawing of what is on the wall.)	(If possible, show a picture of this.)	Watch TIR mime, and if appropriate look at the picture.
But over the years, it has become difficult to make out all the details. The strange thing is, as you know, he did not build this temple.	Treats them as 'experts'.	Realise they are being treated seriously.
But on the walls, there is no painting of the woman who had this temple built for herself, Queen Hatshepsut. I wonder why? Let's have a rest now. Sit down.	*Sounds the cymbal* and goes into role as Queen Hatshepsut.	
'My step-son Tuthmosis is too young to rule. I shall govern the kingdom. And when I die, I wish there to be the most beautiful temple in which I shall lie.	TIR in role.	Listen to the Queen.
The slaves will build the temple. Who will be Senenmut, my principal steward in charge of the building?	Asks for a volunteer. (Be careful! This role is an authority one.)	Those who wish to be challenged volunteer.

Lesson Outline	Teacher Role	Pupil Activity
Now we need (four) groups, each with an overseer.	(Decide on the number of groups in advance — approximately five pupils in each group.) Organises groups and chooses the overseer in each.	Prepare to work in groups.
The ground where my temple is to be built must be cleared of sand and stone.	Sets the context.	
Senenmut! Start your teams working!	Gives responsibility to pupil in role.	Groups work in role.
Now you must build a ramp – up which the large stones will be pulled.	Sets the task.	Organise, negotiate and use mime and movement.
Here are the stones. They have been cut in nearby quarries. Attach ropes to them, and pull them up.	(You can monitor in role, but try and leave the organisation to Senenmut and the overseers.)	Carry on working, each group establishing their space and visualising what they are building.
Now organise the sculptors to carve out stone pictures of the Gods.	Asks for concentration with more careful miming.	Think how they will carry out this task.
The temple is now ready. Well done, my people!	In role, congratulates the workers and admires the temple.	Respond to TIR.
Here is the inner sanctuary.	Defines the new working area.	
And the Goddess I worship, Isis, will live here. Who wish to be the priest and priestess who honour and look after her?	Asks for volunteers to change roles.	New roles adopted.
Only you are allowed into the inner sanctuary. We shall sit and watch while you carry out the ceremonies. First of all bathe yourselves in the Sacred Lake. Now enter the sanctuary. Carefully take the statue of Isis out of her shrine. Sprinkle water on her. Change her clothes. Offer her food and drink. Put her back in the shrine. In the evening close the doors. Go out backwards, brushing away your footprints.	Talks the priest and priestess through the ceremony.	Watch the sacred ceremonies being carried out.
Now, all come out of role.	Brings them out of role.	Respond to instructions.

Lesson Outline	Teacher Role	Pupil Activity
Now Hatshepsut ruled for 20 years – not allowing Tuthmosis to take power. Into threes (A, B and C). A is Tuthmosis. B and C are two members of the court of Hatshepsut. You fear her, but think she has reigned for too long. Tuthmosis – quietly persuade them to help you win the crown which is rightfully yours. Go!	Organises the new groups. Sets the context for work. Starts the role play and monitors the acting out.	Prepare to work in new groups. Adopt new roles.
Who was successful?	Queries.	Respond.
Now, Amun, God of Thebes, was the King of the Gods. If his statue could be placed in the temple, Hatshepsut would have to give the crown to Tuthmosis.	Continues the story.	Listen.
How could this be done, without the priest and priestess of Isis becoming suspicious?	Sets the problem. (The following should only be used if no suitable ideas are forthcoming. If you do not wish the pupils to make the decisions, you should not ask the question above.)	Make suggestions.
Priest and priestess, take up your position outside the sanctuary.	Directs the acting out, defining roles as the action progresses.	Some pupils adopt previous roles and others take on new roles.
Give the priest and priestess a drink, which has a sleeping drug in it. When they fall asleep, quietly creep into the sanctuary and, carefully, because you fear her anger, carry the goddess Isis outside. Others carry the heavy statue of Amun into the sanctuary. Priest and priestess, wake up! What do you see? Hurry to the Queen to tell her.	Talks the acting out through, allowing time for the action to take place.	Respond appropriately to the directions.
I now must give up my throne!	TIR as Hatshepsut. *Sounds the cymbal* to denote change of role and time! Becomes the Chief Archeologist again.	

Lesson Outline	Teacher Role	Pupil Activity
And Tuthmosis so hated her, he banished her from the land. He ordered all the paintings of her on her temple to be painted over and her name was never to be mentioned. Let us pack up our tools now, and we shall leave the temple of Deir-el-Bahari.	Brings the drama to a close.	Listen and respond.
Come out of role.	Establishes an atmosphere for discussion. (Move back to the classroom?)	
Reflection and Evaluation		
Discussion about the ancient temples and tombs of Egypt. This story is based on fact (see list of references). Show pictures if possible.	Leads discussion linked to a topic on Ancient Egypt.	What do they know? What have they learned?
(If appropriate: do you think a descendant of Fankle might have been a Cat God?)	Link to the topic on 'Fankle'.	Hypothesise.

FLANNAN ISLE

Introduction

These three/four lessons can stand alone as a Drama Programme or could be included in a topic such as 'Islands' or 'Mysteries'.

The programme must start off with Lesson One, and you may decide that only this lesson is suitable for your class. If the children are motivated by the mystery, and wish to explore it further, you can decide whether you do both or only one of the following sessions. If doing both, it is immaterial which comes first.

Each lesson uses different types of drama modes or strategies, and it might not be appropriate for the class to attempt each.

Lesson One: Listening, visualising, moving, miming and reporting.
Lesson Two: Group planning, making decisions, acting out.
Lesson Three: Session One consists of group researching and
              planning.
              Session Two is the simulation of a committee of
              enquiry.

Examples of resource material are included, but there are others available. For example, there is a short opera, *The Light House* by Peter Maxwell Davies.

Pupils might have knowledge of their own. I was told by a student from the island of Lewis, that one summer, lights on the now uninhabited Flannans were seen by many reliable people. However, a helicopter sent to investigate found no sign of life.

The class should have some experience of drama. They need concentration and visualisation skills.

You should darken the room, settle the class and read the poem 'Flannan Isle' by WW Gibson with Benjamin Britten's 'Sea Interlude' as a background. Only at the end of the first reading should the class be told that this is a true story, and there should be *no* analysis at this stage. The exploration must begin immediately – while the pictures the poem has evoked are still strong in the children's minds.

There should be an atmosphere of mystery and strange excitement throughout the lesson. Remember, the mystery is in the hands of the children. No-one knows what happened!

Resources

Material about the strange happenings of 1900 can be found in all sorts of books and magazines: from 'Yachting Monthly' to reading schemes such as Ginn.

In *Victorian and Edwardian Highlands from Old Photographs*, selected by F. Thomson (publisher Tantallon), there is a photograph, dated 1895, showing some of the workmen who built the lighthouse. There they are, with a dog and pony, and can provide another good discussion point. Did they experience anything untoward while staying on the island?

I have included here, as part of a 'starter pack', excerpts from *The Scots Magazine* and *Yachting Monthly*, which demonstrate how different information can be given about a true event, which is another interesting point for children to consider. Not all research material might give the correct facts!

Excerpt from 'My Month' by Tom Weir in The Scots Magazine, *describing a journey made by sailing vessel to the outlying islands of the Hebrides.*

That night we anchored in a quiet landlocked corner of Floday Island. By 7 am we were off again, all three sails set for the Flannans, and since visibility was almost nil in the drizzle, I stayed in my bunk for the 20-mile cruise to these 'Seven Hunters', the largest of which was our immediate target, the one bearing the lighthouse whose three keepers mysteriously disappeared in 1900, shortly after it was built. Today the light is automatic, and Eilean More still holds the secret of the missing men. Those who came to investigate the cause of the light going out saw an open door, a table spread for dinner, a chair overturned on the floor but no evidence of what had happened to the men...

We did have time to explore Skiobageo, a deep creek penetrating like a tunnel into the crags near where our dinghy was hauled above the West Landing. (We) were first to go in, entering under a great cathedral arch of vaulted roof echoing with the shrieks of kittiwakes. The chamber became narrower and darker and we were almost hypnotised by the rise and fall of the boat in the swell. In the confined space the slunging sounds were magnified to an almost frightening extent.

At the time of the disappearance of the lighthouse keepers, Lewismen who knew Eilean More gave their opinion that Skiobageo might hold the key to the mystery. They had seen mighty waves burst into the blind tunnel to explode back outwards and rush in a wall of water up the rock face of the West Landing.

The official explanation, by Mr Robert Muirhead of the Northern Lighthouse Board, was not so specific:

> 'I am of the opinion that the most likely explanation of the disappearance of the men is that they had all gone down on the afternoon of Saturday 15th December to the proximity of the West Landing, to secure the box with the mooring ropes etc., and that a large body of water going up higher than they were and coming down upon them swept them away with resistless force.'

Two events confirm that the accident happened on 15 December 1900. The skipper of the *Archer* noted that the lighthouse wasn't shining on that stormy night, and the last entry in the lighthouse log was for 9 am on December 15th. Bad weather delayed the relief vessel, and it was Boxing Day before the *Hesperus* arrived.

An exerpt from 'An Isle Beyond an Isle' by Wallace Clark in Yachting Monthly

Admiralty Chart No 3331, The Flannans, has been part of our thick folio of Scotland for almost 30 years. I have often pulled it out of the chart table at home in the winter, and wondered if we'd ever manage to land on that remote and intriguing group.

Ever since we'd seen their scattered silhouette on the western horizon, at least one of the vital ingredients had not been there – a strong crew, settled weather, good visibility, an absence of swell, or our copy of Robert Atkinson's classic 'Island Going'.

Any explorative skipper who reads his descriptions of the stormy petrels [large seabirds] and the still unsolved mystery of the three missing lighthouse keepers in Wilfred Gibson's poem must long to find more at first hand.

The lighthouse itself is massive, white and orderly. Its bright beam blinks all day now, and the accommodation is securely locked. A workshop lies open, with a smithy and giant bellows indicating ancient self-sufficiency, while the signal locker, from which a red flag would be selected to indicate the east or a yellow one for the south, is all in order. If Northern Lights placed a Visitors' Book here I believe it would be honoured, and fresh interest to the somewhat scanty annals of St Flann's little islands. On this day, there was the faint smell of tar and whitewash, but no sad vibes from the three keepers who disappeared without trace in December 1900, almost exactly a year after the light was established.

Why and how they died remains a mystery. How, above all, could all three have been lost at the same time. It is said an enormous swell can erupt without warning at erratic intervals in quite calm weather off the South Landing. It comes as if by a submarine explosion, and reaches the crane 70 ft up the cliff. As no-one had wintered on the island for centuries, the keepers would not have known of the risk. This is the most probable explanation, but there is room for speculation. The landings were much too far away for a shout to be heard inside. Nowadays, you might guess a UFO had taken them all away. Later another keeper fell off the tower (perhaps terrified by a ghostie), and two more were drowned at the landing. Now the island is owned by the birds. Long may they reign.

Advice for Lesson One It will be important to establish an appropriate atmosphere for this first lesson. The room should be darkened if possible, and the suggested music is needed in the background while the poem is being read.

Background resources can be easily found to add to the interest in the study of the mystery. Children can be encouraged to carry out their own research, but within each drama session they can be told that *their* solutions are all valid – no one knows exactly what happened.

Lesson title

The Poem, Visualisation and Movement

	OUTCOME/ ATTAINMENT TARGET	*STRANDS*
Level: **D** *Key Stage 2 Levels 4–5*	**Using** *materials, techniques, skills and media*	*Investigating and experimenting:* **experiment with space and movement concentrating on the strange situation**
Date:		*Using movement and mime:* **control their movement, accepting the challenge of working 'as if' alone**
Learning Aims: 1 **Investigate a mystery stimulated by a poem** 2 **Use listening and concentration skills** 3 **Make and justify decisions**		*Using language:* **justify their choices and respond to questioning**
Other Information **The first of three lessons on the mystery of the Flannan Isle**	**Expressing** *feelings, ideas, thoughts and solutions*	*Creating and designing:* **adopt the role of investigator and think how that person might react**
		Communicating and presenting: **listen and in turn communicate their reasons for choosing an object**
Resources: **'Flannan Isle' by WW Gibson** **Space** **Tape recorder** **'Sea Interludes' by Benjamin Britten** **Background reference material**		
Organisation 1 **Children seated on floor** 2 **Move independently** 3 **Large circle**	**Evaluating** and **Appreciating**	*Observing, listening, reflecting, describing and responding:* **listen and reflect on all contributions. Decide which three objects will add to their further investigations. Respond to the background information**

FLANNAN ISLE by WW Gibson

Though three men dwell on Flannan Isle
To keep the lamp alight,
As we steered under the lee we caught
No glimmer through the night!

A passing ship at dawn had brought
The news; and quickly we set sail,
To find out what strange thing might ail
The keepers of the deep-sea light.

The winter day broke blue and bright,
With glancing sun and glancing spray,
While o'er the swell our boat made way,
As gallant as a gull in flight.

But as we neared the lonely isle,
And looked up at the naked height,
And saw the lantern towering white,
With blinded lantern, that all night
Had never shot a spark
Of comfort through the dark,
So ghostly in the cold sunlight
It seemed, that we were struck the while
With wonder all too dread for words.

And, as into the tiny creek
We stole beneath the hanging crag,
We saw three queer, black, ugly birds –
Too big, by far, in my belief,
For guillemot or shag –
Like seamen sitting bolt-upright
Upon a half-tide reef:
But, as we neared, they plunged from sight,
Without a sound, or spurt of white.

And still too mazed to speak,
We landed; and made fast the boat;
And climbed the track in single file,
Each wishing he were safe afloat,
On any sea, how ever far,
So it be far from Flannan Isle:
And still we seemed to climb, and climb,
As though we'd lost all count of time,
And so must climb for evermore.
Yet, all too soon, we reached the door –
The black, sun-blistered, lighthouse-door,
That gaped for us ajar.

Yet, as we crowded through the door,
We only saw a table spread
For dinner, meat and cheese and bread;
But, all untouched; and no one there:
As though, when they sat down to eat,
Ere they could even taste,
Alarm had come; and they in haste
Had risen and left the bread and meat;
For at the table-head a chair
Lay tumbled on the floor.

Miss out the next three lines –
children may concentrate
on the bird, rather than the
missing men!
⌈We listened, but we only heard⌉
│The feeble cheeping of a bird │
⌊That starved upon its perch; ⌋

And listening still, without a word,
We set about our hopeless search.
We hunted high, we hunted low;
And soon ransacked the empty house.

Then o'er the Island, to and fro,
We ranged, to listen and to look
In every cranny, cleft or nook
That might have hid a bird or mouse;
But though we searched from shore to shore,
We found no sign in any place;

Miss out the next four lines. Children
will be taking on the roles of adults,
and do not need to be confused by being
suddenly asked to think as children.
⌈And soon again stood face to face ⌉
│Before the gaping door; │
│And stole into the room once more│
⌊As frightened children steal. ⌋

Aye: Though we hunted high and low,
And hunted everywhere,
Of the three men's fate we found no trace
Of any kind in any place,
But a door ajar, and an untouched meal,
And an overtoppled chair.

And, as we listened in the gloom
Of that forsaken living-room –
A chill clutch on our breath –
We thought how ill-chance came to all
Who kept the Flannan Light:
And how the rock had been the death
Of many a likely lad:
How six has come to a sudden end,
And three whom we'd all known as friend,
Had leapt from the lantern one still night,
And fallen dead by the lighthouse wall:

We seemed to stand for an endless while,
Though still no word was said,
Three men alive on Flannan Isle,
Who thought on three men dead.

Lesson Outline	Teacher Role	Pupil Activity
Introduction Children sit at spaced intervals in the drama area. Introduce the idea of listening to a poem.	Organises.	Prepare to listen.
Room is darkened.	Establishes contrast in lighting mood.	
Tape is started.	Establishes atmosphere with music and voice.	Listen.
Poem is read.		
Development 'That was a *true* story'.	Probably surprises the class.	
Background to the Story On 15 December 1900 a ship passing the Flannan Islands reported on arrival in port that there was no light burning; but the relief vessel, *The Hesperus* did not arrive until Boxing Day, 26 December 1900. The men who landed found no trace of the missing lighthouse keepers, and to this day we do not know what happened to them.		
'Now, you each are one of the men from *The Hesperus* sent to find out why the lamp has not been shining forth.	Gives the drama context.	
When I start the music again, you prepare to land, but before we start I am going to ask you to carry this out *without looking at anyone in the room*. There must be no eye contact. You must feel that you are alone on this island. There is a strange atmosphere but you must act bravely.'	Builds in CONTROL mechanism.	Accept challenge of the role.
To the music, talk the class through the actions of the men preparing to land, seeing the strange birds, climbing up the path, feeling apprehension, finding the door ajar, slowly pushing it open, lifting up the upturned chair, exploring the lighthouse, searching the island, returning to the empty room...	Take this section slowly – allowing time for the children to visualise the scene before them, move and to build up tension.	Move about appropriately, showing concentration and commitment to the task.

Lesson Outline	Teacher Role	Pupil Activity
	FADE the music.	
'Look about the room. You can bring back *one* object from the lighthouse. Something that might perhaps give a clue as to what has happened, or something that you think is particularly special...	Sets a task.	Decision making.
Collect it carefully...	Maintains the quiet atmosphere.	Move and mime appropriately.
Now, move into a large circle and sit down with the object beside you.'	Structures space.	Carry their object and place it beside them.
Join the circle.	Becomes part of the group.	All now work as a group.
One by one, the children place their chosen object in the centre of the circle, explaining why they have brought it back with them.	Encourages a ritualistic placing of the objects.	Listen and concentrate as each carries out the task.
Slowly and quietly each object is placed in the circle.	(Do not allow any surface or comic reactions by quietly querying anything that seems to be inappropriate and encouraging sensible reasons to be given.)	Justify why they have chosen to bring the object they have placed in the circle.
'Now we can choose *three* objects, which we might use later in our drama. Which shall we choose?	Gives opportunity for group decision making.	Make and agree on decisions.
When I click my fingers all the objects will disappear, we are back in class and I will tell you more about Flannan Isle.'	(Contrast of voice and movement will change the atmosphere of the session.)	React to teacher's change of approach.
Reflection and Discussion		
Questions: eg Did any anyone know this story already? What must it have been like to land on the island on 26th December 1900?	Leads reflection.	Can they give ideas of their own?
Give out some resource material.	Shows background reference material.	Look at and discuss the different ways the story has been told.

Flannan Isle

Mr John S. Ducat no longer lives at the address given on his letter, but I have been in communication with him. He met James Ducat's daughter, when she was 99 years old in 1991, and she remembered kissing her father goodbye before he went on his last journey to Flannan Isle.
'It was a bright sunny day and James lifted both the children up and kissed them before walking away. The children called out to him and he returned and gave them another kiss and left. Years later Anna would look back and wonder if her father had a premonition of what was to come.'
Anna died in November 1993, aged 101.

---

23 Scar Hill Road
Boylston
Massachusetts, USA

The Scots Magazine
Edinburgh

January 1985

Dear Sir
Tom Weir's September 1984 'My Month' article was of special interest to me. In it he refers to the Flannan Isles lighthouse 'whose three keepers mysteriously disappeared in 1900'. One of the three, and the Principal Keeper, was James Ducat, my grand-uncle, who served the Northern Lighthouse Board for 22 years prior to his untimely death at the age of 44. He left a wife and five children.
I would be interested in anything additional that your readers or contributors could add to my research on these outlying islands of the Hebrides and the secrets of the missing men still held by Eilean More.
Yours sincerely

John S. Ducat

Lesson title

What Happened?

Level: **D**	Key Stage **2** Levels **4–5**

Date:

Learning Aims:
1 **In groups, experiment with ideas**
2 **Evaluate group and individual contributions**

Other Information
The second of three lessons on the mystery of Flannan Isle

Resources:
'Flannan Isle' by WW Gibson
Space
The letter to The Scots Magazine
Music
Percussion

Organisation
1 **Whole class**
2 **Group discussion and rehearsal**
3 **Groups acting out**
4 **Discussion and evaluation**

OUTCOME/ ATTAINMENT TARGET	STRANDS
Using materials, techniques, skills and media	Investigating and experimenting: **in groups, co-operate in the planning of an improvisation** Using movement and mime: **experiment with movement which is appropriate to the action** Using language: **contribute to the planning and use appropriate language within the acting out**
Expressing feelings, ideas, thoughts and solutions	Creating and designing: **plan co-operatively to carry out the drama task** Communicating and presenting: **effectively present their own ideas using speech, movement, gesture, sound effects and props as created and designed**
Evaluating and **Appreciating**	Observing, listening, reflecting, describing and responding: **contribute by reflecting on, evaluating and responding to ALL presentations**

Lesson Outline	Teacher Role	Pupil Activity
Introduction		
Revise the story of Flannan Isle.	Recaptures the atmosphere of the story.	Are enthusiastic to be more involved with the mystery.
Read and/or revise the letter to *The Scots Magazine* by John Ducat.	Focuses attention on a different aspect of the story.	Listen.
Development		
'Now, let us imagine that in the American home of John Ducat, there is a photograph of his ancestor, the James Ducat who disappeared in December 1900.	Sets the drama context.	
One year, on 15 December, he steps out of the photograph and tells the story of what happened that same night, long ago.		
In your groups you are going to act out what happened.	Gives information about their task.	Listen.
You can decide whether *your* James Ducat, as well as beginning the story, also takes part in the action, or someone else can be him on the island.		
Remember, *your* ideas might be the true answer solution to the mystery...		
Divide the class into groups of 3/4 children.	Organises groups and space.	Take up their working areas.
Groups have 5 minutes only to discuss what they think happened and how they wish to represent this.	Checks each group.	Discuss, decide and negotiate.
Groups rehearse their scenes, all working at once.	Moves around groups, making sure they are on their feet and working at the task. Supplies any resources they may need, for example music, percussion, simple props.	Experiment and find a way to *clearly* show their solution to the mystery.
Each group, in turns, acts out its scenes.	Watches, controls if necessary. Makes positive comments at the end of each scene, if they merit it!	Act out, and watch carefully.

Lesson Outline	Teacher Role	Pupil Activity
Reflection and Evaluation Which idea might be the true solution? Did all the groups clearly show what they think happened? 'Do you want to work on them again, improving, not changing what you did before? Do you want to work on *one* of the ideas, thinking of making it like a play for television? If so, what do we all need to do?'	Depending on the results of the acting out, the lesson can end with an evaluative discussion, or could be developed further.	Discuss the ideas and the presentations. Perhaps go on to develop one idea further.

Flannan Isle

Role cards 2–7 will be given out to small groups who can discuss how the characters they represent would speak and act at the enquiry. The *Joseph Moore* card should be given to someone in Group 6, so that he or she can discuss with them what they will say at the enquiry.

The Free Choice card need not be used. If the class is experienced in Drama and have come up with interesting solutions to the mystery, then another group might be represented, if it is appropriate.

1 If the class are used to this method of working the groups can be listed on the board and the children can decide on who they want to be, with further details being given out once they are organised: *or*

2 Number the class two–seven. All the *twos* come together, the *threes*, and so on (this method can divide 'cliques').

Have as many resources regarding Flannan Isle and other lighthouses available. The groups can research the material, so that they have evidence they can bring to the enquiry.

The three objects brought back are placed on Mr Muirhead's desk. If you cannot supply a realistic prop, use a similar article to symbolise it; for example, if a photograph has been brought back, a sheet of paper could be used (the person who chose the photograph can write or draw on it what it is meant to show).

The Enquiry

	OUTCOME/ ATTAINMENT TARGET	STRANDS
Level: D **Key Stage 2** **Levels 4–5** Date: Learning Aims: 1 **Research a topic** 2 **Develop a role within a large group**	**Using** materials, techniques, skills and media	*Investigating and experimenting:* **investigate their roles, and interact within and without the groups** *Using movement and mime:* **decide how their character will react non-verbally** *Using language:* **contribute to the planning through research and discussion, and use speech flexibly, responding to the changing situation while role-playing**
Other Information **Guidance is given on how to organise and manage a simulation.** **This lesson therefore can provide a model on which to base other meetings where the children plan and participate in a simulation exercise.** Resources: **As much background material as possible (see 'The Mystery of Flannan Isle: resources')** **Role cards**	**Expressing** feelings, ideas, thoughts and solutions	*Creating and designing:* **understand the feelings of the people involved in the mystery and work together within the context** *Communicating and presenting:* **decide on effective use of props, speech and movement which will bring the simulation to life**
Organisation **NB two sessions** 1 **Session one – group work** 2 **Session two – formal setting for the enquiry** Open-ended drama 3 **Reflection and evaluation**	**Evaluating** and **Appreciating**	*Observing, listening, reflecting, describing and responding:* **think about this session and the others, and discuss the different types of drama strategies that have been used and come to some conclusions on which they prefer and why. Relate this discussion to comparing their experiences with aspects of the mass media.**

Role Cards

These role cards are given out to each group (see page 51). Ideally each child should have one. He or she can write personal information on the back. Funny or eccentric names should not be used as this will encourage giggles – this is to be a serious exercise carried out with commitment and conviction.

Remember that the teacher is in role as Mr Muirhead, the Superintendent of the Northern Lighthouse Board, and can control with appropriate authority, but can come quickly out of role, bringing the class also out of role to evaluate the situation and judge whether its responses are appropriate.

Role card 1 should also be written on the board so that everyone can see the teacher's role.

Note that multiple copies are required for some of the cards.

Role card 1

Mr Robert Muirhead

Superintendent of the Northern Lighthouse Board

Mr Muirhead has called people interested in the disappearance of the lighthouse keepers to an enquiry. He is an understanding and sympathetic man, but he wishes to find out what happened.
He is trying to find a logical explanation.

Role card 2

A lighthouse keeper

You have served on Flannan Isle Lighthouse, and many others. You know the importance of keeping a log. You knew the missing men.

Role card 3

A local fisherman

You know the area of water around the Flannan Isles. You have landed occasionally in good weather, and knew the missing men. You were fishing in the area in December 1900, but went to port when the weather became really stormy.

Role card 4

A lawyer representing the relations of the lost men

Decide with the other lawyers which of the three men's relatives you are representing. The family wants to know the truth. They do not wish their reputations to come to harm. Who is to blame? Will there be compensation?

Role card 6

The men who landed with Joseph Moore

You are experienced seamen and you have seen many strange things, but you do not understand what happened on the island, although you might have an idea. You may be reluctant to share this with others. You knew the men very well and respected them.

Role card 5

A man who helped to build the Flannan Isles Lighthouse

You were glad to get off the island when the lighthouse was built, but you are not really sure why you were so relieved to get back to the mainland. You know a lot about the landing conditions near the lighthouse.

Role card 7

Local reporters

You represent the papers that all the islanders read. You have heard strange stories about the Flannan Isles, but want to be able to report the *truth!*

Role card

Joseph Moore

You returned to Flannan Isle to take up duty. Your return had been delayed because of bad weather, and you had heard the light was not being lit! The missing men were your good friends. What had happened?

Free choice

If you wish to add another group who might have been present, decide on who they might be and fill in this card.

Drama 5–14 © 1995 Irené Rankin, Hodder & Stoughton

Lesson Outline	Teacher Role	Pupil Activity
First Session (Research and Preparation)		
Introduction		
Remind the class of the exploration of the lighthouse and the island by the men who arrived on 26 December 1900.	Sets the context of mystery.	Prepare to work on the topic.
Which three objects did they choose to bring from the island that might be important in the solving of the mystery? Do they wish to change anything?	Reminds them of previous lesson.	Come to a consensus on the objects they will use.
Development		
The classroom will become the committee room of the Northern Lighthouse Board.	Outline the setting for the work to follow.	Listen.
An enquiry into the disappearance of the lighthouse keepers is going to take place in front of Mr Robert Muirhead, Superintendent of the Northern Lighthouse Board.		
The three objects brought from the island will be on display.		
The men who landed will report on what they found when they landed.		
The class are informed as to who will be present.		
(See advice notes.)		
They are then grouped and given appropriate role cards (see resources).	(Depending on the experience of the class the children can choose which group they wish to be in or the teacher can plan this.)	Go into groups and read their role cards.
Resources and information should be on hand. Supply any knowledge which they require for their roles. NB Keep the historic facts correct: there would have been no electricity or radio, and wireless telegraphy had not been installed on the Island at the time of the keepers' disappearance.		

Lesson Outline	Teacher Role	Pupil Activity
However, Mr Muirhead stated that it would not have made any difference if there had been no communication. People just would have thought that the wireless had failed — not that the three men had disappeared.		
Time allowed for this should be no more than an average drama session (ie about 30 mins).	(Pupils can be encouraged to research and prepare outside of the allotted class time.)	
Second Session: The Enquiry		
The classroom is set up as a committee room where an enquiry can take place. This is a formal setting.	Organises the space.	Help lay out the functional space.
The chosen objects from the island are placed on the desk.		
(See advice notes.)	Starts the drama.	Go into role.
The participants take up their seats.		
Robert Muirhead enters and opens the proceedings.	TIR	Respond to TIR.
Calls on the three men who landed on the island to recount what they found.		
Open Ended		
From this point on the session is in the hands of the participants with the Chairman monitoring the process.	(You hold an authority role, but can also bring the class out of the drama if they are not committed to the task, or forget the restrictions due to historical fact.)	In role, listen to the evidence; challenge it and the witnesses; present own reasoned opinions.
At any point the 'Mr Muirhead' can call for a recess to allow groups to interact or to reconsider the evidence.		
Robert Muirhead can conclude the enquiry with the following words written by him on 8 January 1901.	Decides when it is appropriate to draw the proceedings to a close.	May not be satisfied with the outcome!
'After a careful examination of the place, the railings, ropes etc and weighing all the evidence which I could secure, I am of the opinion that the most likely explanation of the disappearance of the men		

Lesson Outline	Teacher Role	Pupil Activity
is that they had all gone down on the afternoon of Saturday, 15 December, to the proximity of the West Landing, to secure the box with mooring ropes, etc, and that an unexpectedly large roller had come up on the Island, and a large body of water going up higher than where they were and coming down upon them has swept them away with resistless force.' New rules might be drawn up for lighthouse keepers. The mystery can be left researched, but unresolved. The drama is ended.	Brings everyone out of role.	NB Often reluctant to give up their role!
Reflection and Evaluation *Out of role* the class discusses the preceding drama sessions. Out of the three, which did they prefer? Why?	Leads discussion, reminding them they are no longer at the enquiry.	Evaluate the different styles of drama sessions.
Had they moved towards discovering the solution?		Consider their contributions to the investigation of the mystery.

THE DESPERATE JOURNEY

Introduction

Drama can bring the characters in a novel to life. The children 'become' the participants, experiencing some of the feelings and emotions, and through discussing them, come to a better understanding of the motives and reactions of the people who are portrayed in the written word.

In the lessons that follow, only in Lesson Two do the children actually re-enact something they have read. In other lessons they are asked to imagine what *might* happen, and then find out what has been written.

Lesson One	The teacher in role as Patrick Sellar confronts the children.
Lesson Two Countess	(This can be taken in two sessions.) TIR as the talks to the children, who have adopted the role of Sellar. Then the burning of Culmaile is acted out.
Lesson Three	Life in Glasgow. (This session can also be used to illustrate life in Victorian times.)
Lesson Four	This lesson uses mime and movement to show the journey through the ice.
Lesson Five	A meeting where decisions have to be made.

Lesson title

On the Shore

Levels: **D/E**	Key Stages **2/3** Levels **5–7**

Date:

Learning Aims:
1 Experience empathy with Kirsty and Davie

Other Information
The first in a series of lessons that should add to the children's understanding of the novel
NB The drama in this first session should be quite short

Resources:
Chapter One of The Desperate Journey by Kathleen Fidler (see Bibliography on page 105)
The board – to illustrate high- and low-tide marks
Teacher in Role (TIR) as Patrick Sellar

Organisation
Whole group work

OUTCOME/ ATTAINMENT TARGET	STRANDS
Using materials, techniques, skills and media	Investigating and experimenting: **improvise** Using movement and mime: **mime** Using language: **use language appropriately**
Expressing feelings, ideas, thoughts and solutions	Creating and designing: **adopt a role from the novel** Communicating and presenting: **work co-operatively**
Evaluating and **Appreciating**	Observing, listening, reflecting, describing and responding: **listen and reflect on the situation**

Lesson Outline	Teacher Role	Pupil Activity
Introduction		
Read up to the line 'What are you young rascals up to?' on page 10 of the book.	Story teller.	Listen.
Development		
There is an unwritten law of the sea shore.	Gives background to the forthcoming dispute.	
Everything *beneath* the high water mark can be claimed by anybody. *Above* the high water mark it is owned by the landowner.		
Demonstrate on board.	Uses board to illustrate low- and high-tide water.	
Therefore if Davie and Kirsty are collecting *here*...	Indicates *below* high water mark.	Observe.
are they in the right or wrong?	Queries. (Have they grasped the 'law'?)	Respond.
The man is Patrick Sellar. He works for the Countess of Sutherland, who owns the land. So she owns everything... where?	Gives the background information.	Listen.
	Can they work out she owns everything *above* the high water mark?	Respond.
Let's act this out.	Introduces idea of acting out.	
I wonder what Sellar is going to say to the children?		
When I say 'Go!' you will all become Davie and Kirstie collecting mussels and putting them into your creels.	Sets up the context.	Prepare to work.
'Go!'	Starts the acting out.	Use mime.
'What are you rascals up to?'	Goes into role as Patrick Sellar.	React appropriately.
'I am Patrick Sellar, the Countess of Sutherland's factor. You know that I look after her land and all the people on it. You are stealing her ladyship's shellfish!'		

Lesson Outline	Teacher Role	Pupil Activity
Dispute with the children over the right to catch fish below the high-water mark.	Challenges in role.	In role, the children tell of their knowledge of the rules of the sea.
	Judge when it is suitable to end the confrontation. Do not let it carry on for too long!	
End with – 'Your family will pay for this impudence!'		
Freeze!	Stops the drama.	Come out of role.
We'll see now what happened in the book when Patrick Sellar appeared.	Return to the book.	They should be eager to see if what they did is the same as in the book.

The Desperate Journey

Patrick Sellar Carries Out the Countess' Orders

	OUTCOME/ ATTAINMENT TARGET	STRANDS
Levels: D/E **Key Stages 2/3** **Levels 5–7**	**Using** *materials, techniques, skills and media*	*Investigating and experimenting:* **improvise within two situations** *Using movement and mime:* **show ability to adapt movement and mime to suit the situation** *Using language:* **use appropriate language in role**
Date: Learning Aims: 1 **Adopt various roles** 2 **Experience the situations** as if **they were there**		
Resources: **Chapter two of** The Desperate Journey **by Kathleen Fidler (see Bibliography on page 105)** **Teacher in Role (TIR) as** 1: **Countess of Sutherland** 2: **Kate Murray** **Letter (see page 28 in** The Desperate Journey*).*	**Expressing** *feelings, ideas, thoughts and solutions*	*Creating and designing:* **develop roles already experienced** *Communicating and presenting:* **work co-operatively**
Organisation 1 **Read the story** 2 **Whole group with TIR** 3 **Reflection** 4 **Continue the story**	**Evaluating** and **Appreciating**	*Observing, listening, reflecting, describing and responding:* **reflect upon the historical happenings**

Lesson Outline	Teacher Role	Pupil Activity
THE BURNING OF CULMAILIE		
Introduction		
Read up to the line 'Here they come!' Davie exclaimed tensely.	Story teller.	Listen.
Development		
Do you remember when Davie and Kirsty went to the castle, they had to wait a long time before Patrick Sellar appeared?	Asks them to recall.	Recall.
He was being interviewed by the Countess of Sutherland.		
I wonder what she was saying to him? The scene is NOT in the book.		
Let's try to create it now!	Challenges.	
I would like you all to be Patrick Sellar. I am your employer, the Countess. Remember, I can sack you at a moment's notice. You must show me great respect.	Gives out the roles. (There is no reason why there should not be several Patrick Sellars! This method can encourage a shy child to make an opinion heard.)	Prepare to interact with the TIR.
When I click my fingers, you have just entered the Countess' drawing-room.	Sets the context.	
Click fingers.		
'Well – Sellar! What is the position with the crofters?'	TIR (Be prepared to respond seriously to what they say.)	Respond and act out appropriately.
Click fingers.	Controls and stops the drama.	Come out of role.
What do you feel about Patrick Sellar's position? Should we sympathise with him?	Queries.	Can they empathise with Sellar?
What do you think he'll do when he reads the letter?	Queries.	Attempt to forecast events.
Let's find out from the book.	Returns to the written word.	
Continue reading from page 31, repeating, 'Here they come!' Davie exclaimed tensely.		

Lesson Outline	Teacher Role	Pupil Activity
Read on to page 38: '...we must go from here and leave Culmailie for ever.		
The lesson can stop here if there is a lack of time, but for immediate impact, please continue!	(The lesson can be restarted at this same point, but will not be so effective.)	
Do you realise that this is a *true* story? People *were* treated like this.	Creates *tension*.	Building belief in the situation.
It is difficult to imagine what it must have been like. Let's try to put ourselves into their position.	Invites them to participate.	Prepare to adopt roles.
Who will join me, Kate Murray, as part of my family?	Invites volunteers.	Volunteer.
And who will be Patrick Sellar...	Looks for a single volunteer.	
...and his men?	Involves the rest of the class. (No spectators.)	
'Patrick' – you will start by asking for James Murray... 'Davie' – you will hand him this letter.	Directs. Gives 'Davie' a 'real' letter – a prop.	Prepare to improvise.
Go	Knows what Kate does in the story, so that a lead can be given.	Act out appropriately without scripts.
	(Remember the drama can be stopped and discussed if moving away from the story-line.)	
	Includes the curse (page 35).	
When the action has been completed to everyone's satisfaction (page 36; lines 7/8): 'Go on your way! You have done that for which you came!'	TIR brings the acting out to a close.	All respond in the adopted roles.
Freeze.	Controls.	Come out of role.
Reflection and Discussion		
Open questions: eg 'How did those of you who were the men evicting the Murray Family feel?'		
Suggested Activity		
WORD BANK? perhaps leading to a poem?		

Topic *The Desperate Journey*

Lesson title **In the City**

	OUTCOME/ ATTAINMENT TARGET	STRANDS
Levels: D/E Key Stages **2/3** Levels **5–7**	***Using*** *materials, techniques, skills and media*	*Investigating and experimenting:* **improvise and respond to TIR** *Using movement and mime:* **use movement and mime appropriately** *Using language:* **use language appropriately**
Date: Learning Aims: 1 **Adopt various roles** 2 **Experience empathy with the characters in the novel**		
Resources: **Chapter four of** The Desperate Journey **by Kathleen Fidler (see Bibliography on page 105)** **Tambour for control** **TIR as Foreman** **TIR as Landlady**	***Expressing*** *feelings,ideas, thoughts and solutions*	*Creating and designing:* **adopt and develop roles** *Communicating and presenting:* **work co-operatively**
Organisation 1 **Read the story** 2 **Class in two groups, working in an inner and an outer circle** 3 **Reflection** 4 **Whole group work; TIR as Foreman** 5 **Reflection** 6 **Family groups; TIR as Landlady** 7 **Reflection**	***Evaluating*** *and ***Appreciating***	*Observing, listening, reflecting, describing and responding:* **identify and understand the problems**

Lesson Outline	Teacher Role	Pupil Activity
Introduction		
Read to the line 'Nobody seemed to have any use for a man who had once been a farmer' on page 67.	Story teller.	
Recap on the Murray family and their reactions to Glasgow.	Recaps on the book.	Recall what they have read.
Development		
Let us look at another family who might may be facing the same problems as the Murrays.		
The mother and father need work, but there is none available for inexperienced adults. However, they will try to find jobs...	Sets the context.	
Class into two groups: group A are factory foremen, group B are parents.	Directs.	
Group A: make a circle facing outwards.	Organises.	Get into position.
Group B: each go and stand before a foreman.		
Foremen: You are reasonable men. You would like to be able to provide work, but you do not need anybody at the moment. You will begin by being sympathetic, but as the day moves on, you will start to lose your temper.	Gives role background.	Listen and think about how they will respond.
Parents: You *need* work. Your savings are running low and you need to feed your family.		
You will ask for work. Move on to the next foreman at the tambour signal.		
Go.	Starts role play.	Work in role.
Each of Group B tries to get work.		
They move on to the next foreman at the tambour signal.	Controls the activity.	Act out.

Lesson Outline	Teacher Role	Pupil Activity
NB The drama *must* be stopped if they smile or laugh during the role-play. Ask them if this is were a serious situation, would they be smiling? Therefore they must *think* about what they are trying to do.		*Belief* and *commitment* is necessary.
The 'parents' try about four times to get work.		
Freeze and come out of role.	Controls.	
Reflection		
Who might get work and why?	Queries.	Reflect on the situation.
You are all now children working in a factory.	Sets new context.	Prepare to adopt new roles.
What would the conditions be like?	Asks them to think of the environment.	Imagine the situation.
I shall be the foreman. When I sound the tambour, I am beating someone. You start work at 6 am, and I will not have any slackers!	Builds the tension.	
Start work now!	TIR as foreman moves around the class 'bullying' and ejecting to the side (out of the factory) anyone who does not satisfy. (This should move quickly.)	React to TIR.
Freeze and come out of role.	Controls and brings back anyone who had been 'ejected'.	
Reflection		
How would the children feel about the one who was sacked?	Queries.	Empathise.
Let's look at another situation.		
Now, in another Highland family, someone is ill.	Sets new context.	
How would a landlady feel about this?	Queries.	Think about a completely new role.
What could the family do?		
Organise family groups.	Defines space for families NB No babies or young children. (The class must concentrate on the *situation*, not playing at being children.)	Adopt roles.

Lesson Outline	Teacher Role	Pupil Activity
All the families live crowded together in the same house – so you can *hear* what is happening to each family.	Gives directions for the acting out.	Listen.
You will *stay still* until the landlady comes to your room, and will *freeze* when she leaves you, *no matter* what she has said to you.		
What are you going to do when the landlady comes for the rent?	Asks question, but gives no time for consultation.	Prepare individually.
Sit still and quiet and watch what is happening to the families.	Controls.	
'Landlady' deals with each family in turn.	TIR as landlady. (After going to each room, return to one where the family thinks they have got away with it, and evict them!)	Respond to TIR.
Come and sit by me.	Comes out of role.	Come out of role.
What happened and what did you feel about this?	Listens to the reactions.	Reflect on the experience.
I wonder if the Murray family faced these kinds of problems?	Brings the class back to the book.	
Let's go to the book and find out...		

The Desperate Journey

Note:
this diagram shows the
arrangement needed for
the 'pulling the ship'
exercise in the
lesson

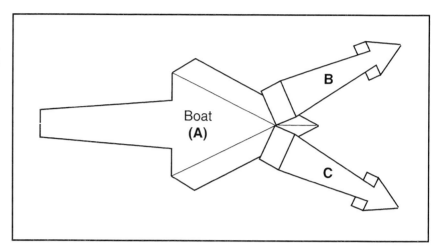

Lesson title

Through the Ice

	OUTCOME/ ATTAINMENT TARGET	STRANDS
Levels: D/E — **Key Stages 2/3** **Levels 5–7**	**Using** materials, techniques, skills and media	Investigating and experimenting: **MUSIC – sing together** Using movement and mime: **PE – demonstrate principles of movement**
Date:		
Learning Aims: **Use music and movement to add to the feeling of effort required for the journey**		
Other Information **See the information on Outcomes/ Attainment Targets and Strands for Music and Physical Education.**	**Expressing** feelings, ideas, thoughts and solutions	Creating and designing: **consider creative use of space** Communicating and presenting: **communicate non-verbally**
Resources: **Chapter Five of The Desperate Journey by Kathleen Fidler (see Bibliography on page 105) Sea shanty: eg Rio Grande Space for movement**	**Evaluating** and **Appreciating**	Observing, listening, reflecting, describing and responding: **evaluate group work**
Organisation **1 The story is read** **2 All sing together** **3 Three groups for movement** **4 Work in small groups** **5 Show the work** **6 Evaluate**		

Lesson Outline	Teacher Role	Pupil Activity
Introduction		
Read to the end of Chapter 5, 'A Way Is Found'.	Story teller.	Listen.
Re-read from page 104: 'When they reached the ship a warmer wind was already blowing...' to page 105: '...and the ship shook out her sails like a lovely bird poised for flight.'		
Development		
All sing a sea shanty (Rio Grande).	Leads the singing.	All sing.
Each sing again, pulling on an imaginary rope.	Directs singing, with movement.	Sing and mime.
Divide into three groups A, B and C.	Organises.	
Group A makes the shape of a boat.	Organises the space.	Become aware of creative use of space.
B and C line up some distance away.		
Group A (the ship), sings the lead.	Directs, but encourages experimentation of movement. There are three groups, but they each must be aware of the other, and the singing should match the movement.	Work co-operatively.
Groups B and C answer with the chorus, as they all pull together.		
The 'ship' maintains a *strong* and *uniform* shape, but slowly moves as the 'sailors' pull.	(Remember to stop the action if need be. You are looking for *quality* in movement and sound.)	
When the end of the song is reached, groups B and C come on board (ie into the midst of Group A.)	Directs.	Continue with the movement.
Haul up the sails.		
Now, experiment with movement to give the impression of a ship sailing.	Encourages experimentation.	Offer suggestions, evaluate their results.

Lesson Outline	Teacher Role	Pupil Activity
Reflection and Evaluation		
In smaller groups, experiment with movement to represent the ship being pulled through the ice, and then freely sailing away.	Allows small group negotiation. Watching groups could provide the background music for the movement of each individual group.	Work together, looking for quality in results.
Evaluation		
Could we believe we were watching sailors working in these dangerous and cold situations?	Asks for critical evaluation.	Evaluate their own and others' work.

The Desperate Journey

Return or Stay?

	OUTCOME/ ATTAINMENT TARGET	STRANDS
Levels: **D/E** Key Stages **2/3** Levels **5–7**	**Using** materials, techniques, skills and media	Investigating and experimenting: **investigate problems through the use of language**
Date:		Using language: **use language creatively and appropriately in role**
Learning Aims: **Through the role play, the children come to an understanding of the difficulties the settlers experienced**		
Resources: **Chapter Eight of** The Desperate Journey **by Kathleen Fidler (see the Bibliography on page 105)** **TIR as settler who wishes to return**	**Expressing** feelings, ideas, thoughts and solutions	Creating and designing: **develop ideas in role** Communicating and presenting: **communicate effectively**
Organisation 1 **The story is read** 2 **Revision of problems** 3 **TIR as settler; children adopt roles** 4 **Meeting** 5 **Conclude the story** 6 **Reflection and discussion**	**Evaluating** and **Appreciating**	Observing, listening, reflecting, describing and responding: **listen to opinions in and out of role and respond to the results of the acting out**

Lesson Outline	Teacher Role	Pupil Activity
Chapter Eight **The Land of Promise** **Introduction** Read to the line "'You will be worse off if you have to winter on the shores of Hudson Bay.'" on page 154.	Story teller.	Listen.
Repeat the reading from page 153: 'At Jack River the settlers gave themselves over to despair.'	Focus on the events they will act out.	
Development Revise *all* the tribulations the settlers have encountered.	Encourages recall.	Recall.
Consider the following: Should we stay? What is there for us here?	Asks them to think of these questions.	
	Teacher goes into role as a settler who wishes to return to Scotland. Calls a meeting to persuade people to return.	Go into role and react to TIR.
An open-ended lesson with each person making his or her own decision. Take a vote... Go back to the book to see what happened to the Murrays and their colleagues.	In role, challenges, listens, negotiates.	Put forward opinions, attempt to solve the problem, make decisions.
Reflection and Discussion Open questions. For example: although this happened long ago, is there anywhere today where people are chased from their homes? Think of the whole world....	Reacts and leads from the children's responses.	

CHILDREN IN WAR

Introduction

The three lessons in this topic concentrate on the Second World War. Lesson One, 'The Evacuees' puts the class in role as children who are suddenly up-rooted from home and parents, and sent to strangers in the country.

In Lesson Two, 'The Resistance Workers', the pupils examine the role of people who risked their lives fighting in an occupied country, and have to deal with a problem which arises.

Lesson Three, 'Into Hiding', is a session which investigates a day in the life of Anne Frank and her family.

Unfortunately children are still suffering because of wars, large and small. By acting out incidents that happened some time ago, can the children start to think of what others in their own age group are experiencing?

This topic can be incorporated into work within Environmental Studies: Social Subjects: Understanding People in the Past.

Lesson title

The Evacuees

	OUTCOME/ ATTAINMENT TARGET	STRANDS
	Using materials, techniques, skills and media	Investigating and experimenting: **interact with TIR developing understanding and knowledge of historical situation**
		Using movement and mime: **show awareness of non-verbal reactions**
		Using language: **use language appropriately and reflect upon and evaluate what has been learned**
	Expressing feelings,ideas, thoughts and solutions	Creating and designing: **show insight and understanding of their roles**
		Communicating and presenting: **communicate their thoughts effectively**
	Evaluating and **Appreciating**	Observing, listening, reflecting, describing and responding: **observe the groups at work and reflect and respond to the issues**

Levels: **D/E**   Key Stages **2/3**
Levels **5–7**

Date:

Learning Aims:
1 **Participate in, in an 'as if' situation, events that many children experienced during the Second World War**
2 **Reflect on these and perhaps relate them to present-day situations**

Other Information
This lesson should be taken in the classroom

Resources:
Sticky labels with children's names
Two sets of family names (supplied)
Paper and pencils
Teacher in various roles (TIR)

Organisation
1 **Two groups**
2 **TIR works with Group A while Group B observes**
3 **Reflection**
4 **Group B writes short letter**
5 **Group B works with TIR**
6 **Reflection and discussion**

Lesson Outline	Teacher Role	Pupil Activity
Introduction		
In 1939, the fear of war was great. Cities expected to be bombed, and so the government decided that children should be sent to the country, out of danger. Not much notice was given. Schools sent a letter home to inform the parents. One suitcase, and a gas mask were all each child could take. Goodbyes to the family were said at the station, and after a very long train journey, tired children were taken to village halls, where they were selected by the people who had volunteered to take the city children into their homes.	Gives background information.	Listen.
What was life going to be like for some of them?		
Let's try to find out!	Encourages participation. Divides the class into two groups. Sticks labels on Group A, using their own names, except for two groups of three, who will be given the labels below.	GROUP A prepare to work. GROUP B will sit and watch.
Development	TIR as a billeting officer.	
Line up! Hurry up! I know you're tired, but I'm tired waiting for you... Hurry up!	Organises Group A to stand in front of the class.	Group A responds and lines up.

These family name cards should be photocopied, cut out and given to the two selected groups of three children

```
┌─────────────────┐   ┌─────────────────┐
│                 │   │                 │
│    FAMILY A     │   │    FAMILY B     │
│                 │   │                 │
│                 │   │                 │
│  Emily, aged 14 │   │  Henry, aged 13 │
│                 │   │                 │
│ George, aged 10 │   │ Patricia, aged 9│
│                 │   │                 │
│ William, aged 8 │   │  Mary, aged 7   │
│                 │   │                 │
└─────────────────┘   └─────────────────┘
```

Lesson Outline	Teacher Role	Pupil Activity
Now, these kind people are going to take you into their homes.	Indicates to the right. Moves to the right, and returns as a caring person.	
Oh, you poor dears! I wish I could take you all, but I'll take the youngest. Who is that? Come with me – I've tea all ready.	Walks up and down the line. Cannot take more than one, so takes the youngest who is not part of a family group. Takes the child to his or her seat. Returns as a shopkeeper.	React to TIR. The youngest in the group volunteers the information. Youngest returns to his or her place.
I need two assistants to help in my shop. I'll pick two who look honest and who can count, and I'll have no thieving...	Sets two simple mathematical questions and chooses two children. Returns as a farmer.	The two who satisfy the shopkeeper go with him or her, and return to their seats.
They don't look very strong. I want three boys who can carry bales of hay and bags of corn – but who don't eat too much.	Walks up and down. Finally chooses three. Returns as a bad-tempered person. Goes to a family group. Looks at the eldest.	React to TIR. React to TIR.
You look intelligent and quiet. I'll just take you!	Responds to the family's reaction – refusing to take all three. (Make your own decision as to what you will do!) Returns as a lonely person.	Family should refuse to be separated.
What a nice lot of children! Come away home with me! There's soup waiting for you, and hot water bottles in your beds.	Goes to the other family group.	React to TIR. Go back to their seats.
Come out of role everyone. Sit down.	Directs.	Come out of role.
What did you think about what we were showing you?	Turns to Group B.	
Discussion.		Group B responds.
And what did you think was going to happen to you?	Includes Group A.	
Discussion.		Group A responds.

Lesson Outline	Teacher Role	Pupil Activity
	Issues Group B with paper and pencils.	
Now act as if *you* (indicates Group B) are children who have been evacuated. Some of you will be in good and kind homes – others will have unpleasant experiences – being treated *not* as one of the family, but as servants.	Gives background information.	Listen.
Write a *short* letter home, telling of your experiences.	Moves around Group A asking what they might write if asked. *(Suddenly turns on Group B!)*	Group B writes. Group A discusses with teacher.
What are you writing? How dare you write without showing me!		React to TIR.
	Goes to one who obviously does not wish to show his or her letter.	
Show me! How dare you write this nonsense! I've taken you into my home, fed you and looked after you. This is the thanks I get!		
Freeze.	Controls.	
What could these children do about a person like that?	Leads discussion.	Make reasonable suggestions.
One girl was told by her mother that if she and her three sisters were in trouble, she had to write 'God Save the King' at the end of her letter home, and she used this secret code after being beaten by the eldest daughter of the family with whom they were staying; so her parents sent rail tickets, which allowed them to come home.	Gives background information. (Source: *Evacuees – Scottish Memories,* October 1993)	Listen.

Suggested Continuation

Reflection and Discussion

This was a long time ago in 1939, and also in 1941, during the Second World War. Where are children going through this kind of nightmare now?

Children in War

Note:
this is the coded message
needed for the lesson. Four
copies will be needed.
(The solution may be found
by reading each word
backwards in turn.)

```
ROTIART NI RUO PUORG.
SREIDLOS THGUAC GNIEB DESSAP NWOD
EPACSE ENIL.
NOITAMROFNI EMAC MORF EREH.
LLA EMOC OT EHT NWOT LLAH.
LLET EHT SNAMREG GNISSUCSID HCRUHC
LAVITSEF.
```

Lesson title

The Resistance Workers

	OUTCOME/ ATTAINMENT TARGET	STRANDS
Levels: **D/E** Key Stages **2/3** Levels **5–7**	**Using** materials, techniques, skills and media	Investigating and experimenting: **in a variety of ways, develop an understanding of the work of resistance fighters**
Date:		Using movement and mime: **use clear mime to demonstrate tasks and movement appropriate to the situation**
Learning Aims: **1 Experience in an 'as if' situation, life in an occupied country 2 Consider why people might become traitors**		Using language: **use speech flexibly to respond to changes in the situation and evaluate what has been learned**
Other Information **A section of this lesson could be videoed if equipment is available, and the group enactments evaluated by the participants, but it should be noted that this is not the prime aim of this lesson.**	**Expressing** feelings, ideas, thoughts and solutions	Creating and designing: **plan and implement collaborative group work, and experiment with role in a large group situation during the meeting called by the TIR**
Resources: **Space Percussion (for sound effects) Four copies of the coded message (see above) Tape recorder Recording of marching feet (BBC sound effects record) (If required) video camera**		Communicating and presenting: **use speech, movement, gesture and 'props' appropriate to the task to present a clear picture of the work involved**
Organisation **1 Discussion 2 Group discussion followed by rehearsal of acting out 3 Presentations 4 Groups decode message 5 Whole group meeting interrupted by tape recording 6 Reflection**	**Evaluating** and **Appreciating**	Observing, listening, reflecting, describing and responding: **respond and reflect upon the issue and evaluate their own contribution to it. Identify key elements of what has been experienced and learned.**

Drama 5–14 © Irené Rankin, Hodder & Stoughton

Lesson Outline	Teacher Role	Pupil Activity
(NB The class should know some details of the work of the Resistance before commencing this lesson.)		
Introduction		
Today we are going to look at the work of those people who fought in the Resistance in occupied countries during the Second World War.	Sets the context.	
What kinds of things did they do?	Questions.	Recall previous knowledge.
How would they go about these tasks?		
Sometimes, children of your own age would be involved. What could *you* have done that might not have been quite as dangerous?	Asks them to hypothesise.	
Today I am going to ask you to be older than you are. You will be old enough to carry out the really dangerous tasks.	Introduces the roles they will adopt.	Prepare to adopt roles.
I shall be in role as your Liaison Officer, the person who organises all the resistance activities in the area.	Informs them of teacher's role.	
There are *four* resistance groups in this area.	Chooses four leaders. (NB If the group is inexperienced in drama, do not force girls and boys to work together.)	Each leader chooses their group.
Development		
Groups discuss what is their particular involvement in the resistance.	Out of role, moves around, listening and giving support where necessary.	Group discussion.
	TIR explains that they each have been asked to make a training film for future resistance workers, who are at the moment in England.	Move into acting-out mode.
	They must rehearse for the film.	
		Work out and rehearse their film scenario.
	Moves around groups, finding out what they are doing.	

Lesson Outline	Teacher Role	Pupil Activity
	(During monitoring of their preparations, check if they will need sound effects, of which the teacher will be in charge!)	
It is the day of filming.	Directs, in role. Supplies effects if required.	Each group acts out, as though for a film, what they do within the Resistance.
	(Videos, if a camera *is* being used; in which case, an observer helps with the sound effects.)	
	When all have performed, congratulates them.	
	In role, introduces the *tension* of the coded message.	Listen.
	Hands out a copy of the message to each group (see resources). Out of role, gives help, only where necessary.	Groups decode the message.
Groups, come to the hall, slowly and carefully.	TIR organises journey to the hall (NB They *must* sit in chairs for this meeting as they are adults.)	In role, move to the space designated as the hall. (NB Commitment to role should be strong.)
Please check that there is no one listening outside!	Chooses someone to check.	Feel the tenseness of the atmosphere.
You all know why we are here. I would not normally call you all here together, but you must realise what the message means.	TIR starts the meeting.	Listen and react appropriately.
There is a traitor here in our midst!	*(Real dramatic tension.)*	
What can we do about this?	*From here on,* TIR must take the lead from the participants.	Realise the danger of the situation, and try to solve the problem.
Open-ended.	All suggestions should be treated with seriousness, and inappropriate ideas rejected with good reasons.	
	(There is not too much danger in the situation. However, when you feel the situation has played itself out put on the tape of marching feet.)	
	Starts the tape.	React.
Someone has informed on us! The soldiers are coming!		Holds the tension with the use of voice.

Lesson Outline	Teacher Role	Pupil Activity
	Long pause.	
	Stops the tape.	
	Comes out of role, relaxes the class and brings it out of role.	(This may take some time! If really involved, the children will be reluctant to come out of role.)
Reflection and Evaluation		
Suggested questions:		
Might an incident like this have happened during the war?	Leads discussion.	Respond, using previous knowledge.
What might make a person become a traitor?	Depending on the answers, demonstrate that freedom of choice in an occupied country was not easy.	Predict and project.

Evaluation of Work on Video

If you have been able to video the Resistance Workers demonstrating their work, do not show it to the class until another session. There must be no distractions from the Drama of the Secret Meeting, followed by the discussion on the difficulties in an occupied country.

The video needs to be shown *twice*. There will probably be laughter on the first viewing, especially if the children are not used to the video camera being used in the classroom. Before the second viewing, ask the children to watch, and then answer the following questions, plus any others that you feel need to be asked:

1   Would watchers understand what was happening?
2   If speech was used, could you hear it?
3   If mime was used, were the actions clear?
4   How could your own performance be improved?

This should be followed by a shared evaluation, with the *positive* results being stressed.

Children in War

After May, 1940, good times rapidly fled: first the war, then the capitulation, followed by the arrival of the Germans. That is when the sufferings of us Jews really began. Anti-Jewish decrees followed each other in quick succession. Jews must wear a yellow star, Jews must hand in their bicycles, Jews are banned from trams and are forbidden to drive. Jews are only allowed to do their shopping between three and five o'clock and then only in shops which bear the placard "Jewish shop". Jews must be indoors by eight o'clock and cannot even sit in their own gardens after that hour. Jews are forbidden to visit theatres, cinemas and other places of entertainment. Jews may not take part in public sports. Swimming baths, tennis courts, hockey fields and other sports grounds are all prohibited to them. Jews may not visit Christians. Jews must go to Jewish schools, and many more restrictions of a similar kind.

Margot and I began to pack some of our most vital belongings into a school satchel. The first thing I put in was this diary, then hair-curlers, handkerchiefs, school books, a comb, old letters; I put in the craziest things with the idea that we were going into hiding. But I'm not sorry, memories mean more to me than dresses.

Into Hiding: the Diary of Anne Frank

OUTCOME/ ATTAINMENT TARGET	STRANDS
Using materials, techniques, skills and media	Investigating and experimenting: **develop knowledge and understanding of the situation of the persecuted in an occupied country**
	Using movement and mime: **use movement and gesture showing commitment to the role**
	Using language: **use speech flexibly in role responding to relationships and evaluate what has been learned**
Expressing feelings, ideas, thoughts and solutions	Creating and designing: **demonstrate authenticity in the role-playing, showing an understanding of the situation and how people might react**
	Communicating and presenting: **communicate effectively during group work and discussion**
Evaluating and **Appreciating**	Observing, listening, reflecting, describing and responding: **identifying key elements of what has been experienced and learned**

Levels: **D/E**   Key Stages **2/3**
                     Levels **5–7**

Date:

Learning Aims:
1 **Experience the claustrophobic experiences of people in hiding**
2 **Reflect on these**

Other Information
This lesson need not be used with the book, as readings are supplied

Resources:
Space in which to recreate the living areas
Two readings from The Diary of Anne Frank (given above)
Large cards for each group
Pens or pencils

Organisation
1 **Class group**
2 **Pair work**
3 **Groups of about eight in defined areas**
4 **Reflection and discussion**

Lesson Outline	Teacher Role	Pupil Activity
Introduction		
	Introduce the context by giving the background to the Jews in Holland in 1939.	Listen.
Reading 1.	Reads. (Gives background to Anne's story.)	
Reading 2.	Reads.	
Development		
If *you* had to leave home and did not know when you were returning – what would *you* take and why?	Sets the problem.	Consider the problem.
You are allowed to take only three items. In twos, explain to a partner why you are taking these things.	Organises pairs. Explains the task.	Work in pairs.
Now, into groups of *eight*.	Organises.	Move into larger groups.
	Gives out large card to each group.	Prepare to work together.
List the things being brought (ie 24 items), and strike off duplicates.	Instructs.	Negotiate and co-operate.
You have to get down to 16 items – to be shared amongst the group.		
	Organises three fairly small defined areas.	
Now here are three living areas which will be your home for a long time.	Defines their working areas.	
Work out your space, which has to be for night-time, as well as for during the day.	Directs.	
		Groups plan their living areas.
I will call out the times of the day.	Sets the background for their work.	Realise the problem and think how they will cope with this.
During the times when people may be in the office below, there must be silence. Listen carefully, you are going to live through *three* days.	Creates the *tension* of the moment.	
As I call out the times during the day, carry out the appropriate activities...		

Lesson Outline	Teacher Role	Pupil Activity
8.30 am – 12.30 pm	Leads the groups through a day.	Act out the day's events.
Think about and do things that you can do silently.		
12.30 — 1.30 pm		
Lunch, and you can move about freely.		
1.30 — 5.30 pm		
Silence.		
5.30 — 9 pm		
Evening, and a certain amount of freedom.		
9 pm		
Arrange bedtime space.		
Repeat the day's activities twice more.	Leads through the repeat days.	Do events change?
Freeze and come out of role.	Brings them out of role.	Come out of role.
Reflection		
The Franks and their friends were in hiding from July 1942 until August 1944. What must it have been like?	Leads discussion.	Reflect and talk about the situation.

THE SEA

The lessons within this topic are each for a different stage in the school.

'Trip to the Seaside' (Level A/B) encourages simple mime and movement skills but introduces an element of danger, which should stimulate interest and involvement, and also provides an opening into the study of tides.

Tides are also a part of the lesson in 'The Seal People' (Level C) which is based on a Scottish folk tale. The pupils will be involved in a fantasy lesson, for which they will need to concentrate and suspend belief.

'The Bridge Question' (Level D/E) can become as ambitious as you wish. The first session is devoted to the class becoming involved in its roles and the difficult situation in which it finds itself. Research into the topic should be encouraged, and may involve other areas of the curriculum. During the second session, which starts as a simulation, dramatic tension is introduced, the drama is stopped, and the activity can then be pursued in many different directions.

Lesson title # *A Trip to the Seaside*

Levels: **A/B** Key Stage **1** Levels **1–3**	OUTCOME/ ATTAINMENT TARGET	STRANDS
Date:	**Using** materials, techniques, skills and media	Investigating and experimenting: **within a secure environment pupils will experiment with mime and movement and will solve a problem**
Learning Aims: 1 **Introduce mime skills** 2 **Respond to a dangerous situation**		Using movement and mime: **various different types of movement will be encouraged and simple contrasts of mood will be shown**
		Using language: **appropriate language will be used during the 'rescue' section**
Other Information **This may be the first time 'mime' has been formally introduced. Ther teacher leads the action throughout, encouraging active participation. Tension is introduced moving the lesson away from a movement session into an exciting drama context.**	**Expressing** feelings, ideas, thoughts and solutions	Creating and designing: **pupils will provide solutions and decisions** Communicating and presenting: **communicate ideas**
Resources: **Space**		
Organisation 1 **Whole group responding to teacher's action** 2 **One child volunteers to send for help** 3 **Class discussion**	**Evaluating** and **Appreciating**	Observing, listening, reflecting, describing and responding: **reflect and talk about their drama experience, and the 'performance' of their rescuer**

Lesson Outline	Teacher Role	Pupil Activity
Introduction		
Let's all think of going on a trip to the seaside today!	Introduces the context.	
What kinds of things will we take on a trip?	Questions and accepts appropriate responses.	Respond appropriately.
How will we carry all these?	Questions.	Respond.
Let's pick out the most important things and put them in a bag.	Directs mimed activity.	Mime putting the chosen objects in a bag.
Development		
Now sit quietly with eyes closed.	Settles the class.	
'One, two, three, and here we are, sitting on the sand!'		
	Prepares the class for acting out.	
Now, this is Drama Time, so we can *mime* taking off shoes, sandals and socks.	(Do the children know what 'mime' is? If not, here is an opportunity to explain, demonstrate and introduce drama terminology.)	Demonstrate, or not, knowledge of miming.
We can wriggle our toes in the sand. It feels just like when we run the sand through our fingers in the sand table.	Encourages them to think of an experience they all know.	Try to recreate a sensation.
I'd like to go for a paddle. Are you coming with me?	Encourages active participation.	(Are they all willing to participate?)
But first of all we've got to step through the pebbles, which are sharp.	Leads the movement.	Follow the teacher's lead.
Thank goodness that's over!	Shows relief through use of voice and movement.	Respond.
Here we are at the edge of the water.	Encourages belief and commitment in the situation.	
Dip your toe in – Oh – it's cold!	Leads the mime and shows reactions.	Follow the teacher's lead.
But let's be brave! Step in up to your ankles... Now, up to your knees.		
Look – over there is someone selling ice-cream!	Introduces new interest.	Respond.

Lesson Outline	Teacher Role	Pupil Activity
Out of the water – Over the pebbles –	Leads the movement.	Follow the teacher.
And what would you like?	TIR as ice-cream seller. Leads the action of licking from cones or wafers.	Gather around and choose ice-creams. Mime.
Put on your shoes/sandals.		Respond.
Let's explore the rocks.	Introduces another idea.	
Go carefully! We have to climb over the large ones. The seaweed makes some rocks slippery.	Encourages concentration and careful movement.	Move carefully.
Here is a rock pool. Dip your fingers in. Pick out shiny stones from the bottom. Lay them out in a row on a flat rock. Count how many you have.	Encourages fine motor skill movement as a contrast to previous movement.	Show concentration.
Wait a minute!	Introduces tension with the use of voice.	Stop what they are doing to listen.
Listen! The sound of the sea is getting louder. Oh! Look! The tide has come in! The sea is now between us and the shore. We can't get back! All come close together.	Quickly shows the seriousness of the situation. Discourages suggestions of swimming to the shore!	React appropriately.
Who could rescue us?	Queries.	Make suggestions.
As this is Drama Time, one of you can become a person on the beach who sees what is wrong.	Leads towards the idea of a volunteer who can telephone for help.	
Who wants to be that person?	Picks a reliable child for the first time the lesson is carried out.	Volunteer.
What will — do, when he/she sees us waving?	Queries.	Respond.
(The volunteer stands to one side and is guided through the actions of dialling 999 for the Coastguard or the Police.)	Guides the solo performer.	Volunteer carries out the call while the rest watch and listen.
Look! Here is the life-boat coming to rescue us! Climb on board. Now we're safely back on land!	Leads the class through the rescue.	Move and react.

Lesson Outline	Teacher Role	Pupil Activity
Thank goodness! Thank you, — for telephoning for help.	Shows relief and gratitude.	React with the teacher.
When I click my fingers, we are no longer at the seaside, but back in the classroom. One, two, three – click.	Prepares for them to come out of the drama.	
Sit down.	Settles the class down.	
Discussion		
Well, what an adventure!	Leads reflective discussion.	
But we did something dangerous. What was that? If we were *really* at the seaside and we wanted to explore the rocks, what should we keep doing?		Consider the experience.

The Sea

Note: The text of 'The Story of the Seal Woman' is given at the end of the drama lesson.

The Seal People

Levels: **C/D**	Key Stage **2** Levels **3–5**

Date:

Learning Aims:
1 **Work independently although in a large group**
2 **Experience fantasy and real-life roles**
3 **Work with sensitivity**
4 **Interact appropriately**

Other Information
This lesson could be included in a Scottish programme, or one based on mystery and fantasy

Resources:
Appropriate atmospheric music (eg 'Sea Interludes – Moonlight' by Benjamin Britten
Cymbal
'The Story of the Seal Woman' (supplied)

Organisation
1 **Whole group work with own chairs in plenty of space**
2 **Pair work**
3 **Whole group discussion and reflection**

OUTCOME/ ATTAINMENT TARGET	STRANDS
Using materials, techniques, skills and media	*Investigating and experimenting:* **experiment with various styles of movement, mime and language**
	Using movement and mime: **use a wide variety of imaginative movement in role with confidence and sensitivity**
	Using language: **use language appropriately in role**
Expressing feelings, ideas, thoughts and solutions	*Creating and designing:* **adopt roles and act out appropriately**
	Communicating and presenting: **communicate with and react to a partner**
Evaluating and *Appreciating*	*Observing, listening, reflecting, describing and responding:* **listen and respond to others and reflect on their experiences**

Lesson Outline	Teacher Role	Pupil Activity
Introduction		
Inform the class that they are being asked to do something quite difficult. Are they prepared to try?	Challenges.	Agree to try.
They will all be working together but *must not look* at each other, and the lesson will start with everyone having his or her eyes closed.	Sets the task.	
The class spreads out. If possible, for a feeling of security, the children can take a chair, which they can sit beside and lean on.	Organises the space. Quietly – starts to set the atmosphere.	If possible, take a chair, and sit on the floor beside it.
The class settles down quietly.		
Silence.	Creates the atmosphere for the lesson.	Wait expectantly.
'Close your eyes.'		
Start the music.		
Listen to the sound of the sea. Slowly you are turning into a piece of seaweed attached to a rock.	Quietly paints the picture – bringing them into role.	Listen to the music. Throughout this following section the class are responding to the teacher's voice and visualising what is happening.
As the sea moves around you, you move and undulate with it. And as the tide goes out, you lie against the rock, still and damp...		
Still keeping your eyes closed, slowly you will change now – into a seal... Lying basking against the rock.		Moving appropriately.
Feel the sun on your back; stretch, and feel the sun on your face.	Watches the class, giving them time to move.	Continue to work with eyes closed.
Relax, seals, into a comfortable position.		
Development		
A strange thing happens.	Changes voice.	
Once every 10 years, the seals can cast off their skins and become like human people.	Slows down slightly to build *tension* into the session.	

Lesson Outline	Teacher Role	Pupil Activity
This is the time when it can happen.		
Slowly wriggle out of your skins.	Leads the action.	Start to move.
Open your eyes. *Do not look at anyone.*	Reminds them of the challenge.	
Try standing up. Your legs feel very strange.	Move this part on more quickly – giving little time to be self-conscious.	
Try taking a few steps.		
Wriggle your toes in the sand. Look into a rock pool and imagine what you can see.		
Remember your seal skin. Without it you cannot return to the sea. Hide it away carefully!		
	Starts using space. Gives time for skin to be hidden, and then quickly tell them what is happening.	React and move appropriately.
Someone is coming! You must hide!		
Freeze!	*Controls* the action. *Stops the music.*	
Sit down.		
Now the villagers often come down to the beach to collect things that might be washed ashore. Objects that they might find useful.	Carries on with the 'story'. Changes tone of voice, which should bring the class out of role.	
What kinds of things might these be?	Questions.	Do they know what might be found?
Now, there is an unwritten law for people who live by the sea.	Imparts probable new knowledge.	
If someone finds an object that they want to keep, but for some reason cannot take it home with them immediately, then they can place it *above* the *high water mark*, so that the sea cannot wash it away. This is a sign that it has been claimed, and no other person can take it.		

Lesson Outline	Teacher Role	Pupil Activity
Today, the villagers are coming down to the beach, perhaps to collect something, or to look for useful things.		
All become villagers. You can chat to each other – help each other – what is there on the beach today? The seal people are hiding, so you do not know they are there.	Gives class new roles.	
Go!		Become villagers. Move and talk appropriately, using their chairs as props.
Freeze!	*Controls* the action.	
Take a partner and sit down.	Depending on class experience, the teacher may have to organise the pairing.	
Decide who will be the villager and who will be the seal person.		Pupils negotiate roles.
Seal people are very curious. They are shy, but want to find out what the humans are like, and what they are doing.	Gives guidance as to what each character might be feeling.	The pupils know which role they have adopted. As they listen, they can be mentally preparing on how they might react and what they might say.
The villagers will become conscious that they are being watched.		
Who is the person dressed all in grey?		
Has he or she been shipwrecked?		
How did he or she get to the island?		
Gradually the two will come together...		
The seal person can speak the language of the islander.		
Get into starting positions.		
Villagers – working on the beach; and seal people – watching them.		
Go!	Starts the acting out.	Pair work.

Lesson Outline	Teacher Role	Pupil Activity
(Seal people and villagers talk to each other.)	Watches, monitoring the action, assessing involvement and reactions. Judges *when* to stop the action.	Act out - choosing when to speak to each other. Reacting and responding, each trying to find out about each other.
Freeze.		
But as the sun goes down, the seal people realise that if they do not get back into their skin and return to the sea before sunset – they will be trapped for 10 years.	Sets the challenge of tension and time.	
Do they want to stay? Maybe they do.	Gives opportunity for choice.	
I will give the signal that the sun is going down by striking the cymbal.		
Villagers, are you going to persuade them to stay?		There is no time given for pair discussion, so each must react spontaneously.
(*Sound the cymbal.* Slowly and quietly at first. Take your time from the class's reactions.)	Starts to bring the time element into play.	The seal people realise they do not have long before they should go.
(Build up into a crescendo then *stop.*)		Action may speed up.
Freeze.	Freezes them into tableau position.	
The sun has gone down – relax.		
When I count to three and click my fingers, you are no longer on the island – but back in the classroom. One, two, three, click.	Brings them out of role.	Come out of role.
Final Activity		
Gather the class around. In turn they relate what happened and how they felt about it.	Organises reflection and discussion.	Recount and listen to experiences.
Tell the story of the Silkie, or Seal Woman.		

Suggested Follow-up Activities:

Drama
The villagers visit the seal people under the sea.

Art
Collage work.
Face-painting.

Music
Create sea/seal music.

Dance
As a seal, change to being human, then return to being a seal again. Highland dancing.

Dance/Drama
Villagers encounter the seal people; one is left behind on land.

Environmental Education
What else can the sea give us? How does refuse get on to the beach? What is your local beach like? Can you find out from where the things you find have come?

Language
Sea poetry.
Sea legends.

The Seal Woman

adapted from a Scottish legend by
Irené Rankin

People who live on the islands off the West Coast of Scotland believe that sometimes the seals *do* cast off their skins, and come ashore as people. They tell the story of a seal maiden who came ashore long ago, put her skin to one side, and lay enjoying the sunlight on the beach. She did not know that a young fisherman had seen her swim ashore, and he fell in love with the girl with long golden hair.

He crept down to the beach and stole her seal skin. She was heartbroken when she went to return to her home. She searched high and low, but could not find the means by which she could return home – her seal skin.

She met the young fisherman. There was nowhere she could go, and he was kind and loved her very deeply, and so she married him.

The years passed by and they had two children. They often wondered why their mother looked so sad when she stood on the cliffs, gazing out to sea, but she would never tell them why.

One day, when the fisherman was out at sea, the children were playing in the croft. They lost their ball down the back of a chest of drawers and when they moved it out of the way – they found a piece of what looked like grey material.

'Look what we've found!' they called to their Mother.

She recognised it immediately – it was her seal skin.

Her heart was torn in two. She loved her children and her husband dearly, but the call of the sea and of her people was too great.

'I have to leave you,' she said to the children. 'But if you come to the cliffs or the beach, and sing the song I will teach you, I will hear you and I shall come and see you.'

They did not understand what she was saying, but learned the song and watched her take the grey material and disappear into the night.

The fisherman was distraught when they told him on his return what had happened, but there was nothing he could do.

The children often went down to the shore, and with their song, signalled to their mother, who came and spoke to them, telling them how much she loved them, but how much happier she was now with her own people.

And even today, they say that if you sing a certain kind of music, the seals will come and listen to you, remembering the story of the Seal Woman and her children.

The Sea

Note:
The following lessons,
The Bridge Question *parts 1 and 2*
can be used to include outcomes
and strands from other areas of
the curriculum. Some ideas
for English Language and
Environmental Studies are
given here, but many others
are possible.

ENGLISH LANGUAGE
OUTCOME/   STRANDS
ATTAINMENT TARGET

Writing	Imaginative writing: **imagine life either on the mainland or the island**
Talking	Conveying information: **talk about their attitudes**
	Talking in groups: **ask and answer questions; show awareness of feelings; show audience awareness**

ENVIRONMENTAL STUDIES

Depending on how the drama develops, many aspects within Environmental Studies could be included: the history of the vessel; the effects of the publicity on the Nature Research; 'green issues'; the technology behind the production of a TV programme.

Lesson title

The Bridge Question (1)

OUTCOME/   STRANDS
ATTAINMENT TARGET

Levels: **D/E**	Key Stages **2/3** Levels **5–7**

Date:

Learning Aims:
1 **Research a topic**
2 **Develop a role and understand the attitudes and opinions experienced**
3 **Explore and develop the issues that arise using different drama strategies**

Resources:
Role cards (supplied)
Paper for writing task
Letter from the Chief Inspector

Organisation:

Session One – Group work
1 **Each member carries out writing task**
2 **In role compare notes**
3 **Research and collaborate**

Using materials, techniques, skills and media	Investigating and experimenting: **in role, opinions and attitudes are investigated**
	Using language: **in role, writing and talking tasks are related to the drama topic** (see Outcomes and Strands – ENGLISH LANGUAGE)
Expressing feelings, ideas, thoughts and solutions	Creating and designing: **demonstrate awareness of authenticity in role play and share observations during planning**
	Communicating and presenting: **be actively involved in collaborative planning**
Evaluating and **Appreciating**	Observing, listening, reflecting, describing and responding: **reflect upon the differing opinions of those whose lives will be affected and respond to these in role**

Lesson Outline	Teacher Role	Pupil Activity
FIRST SESSION: Introduction Today our drama will start to examine an environmental problem. Here is the situation: Inverbrae is a village somewhere on the coast. It is a small village but an important one, because the road through Inverbrae leads to a small harbour where the ferry runs between the mainland and the island of Scaravoe. However, it has been suggested that a road bridge a mile long will be built to connect the island and the mainland.	Introduces the context.	Listen.

Role cards

Inverbrae **Hotel Keeper/ Shopkeeper** You will lose trade, especially if a bypass road is built	*Inverbrae* **Ferryman** Your family has run the ferry for generations. You see no prospects of work if the bridge is built.	*Inverbrae* **Nature Reserve Representative** If the bridge is built, fish, animals and birds will be endangered, as the proposed building site is close to the reserve where rare birds and otters breed.
Scaravoe **Hotel Keeper/ Shopkeeper** The bridge will bring more tourists. You can see your business prosper.	*Scaravoe* **Landowner** You are proposing to build a leisure centre and a marina. The bridge will mean prosperity.	*Scaravoe* **Crofter** Life is expensive on the island. Although the bridge is a toll bridge, it will mean cheaper goods, and your own journeys to the mainland will be easier.

Lesson Outline	Teacher Role	Pupil Activity
A new road will bypass Inverbrae, and all traffic will now travel directly to Scaravoe, without having to transfer to the ferry. The idea of the bridge upsets as many people as those whom it pleases. A public enquiry has been called and all those interested and involved are invited to attend.		
Development	Organises groups.	Sit in groups.
In your groups you will each receive a role card which will tell you a) who you are, and b) how you feel about the proposed bridge.	Outlines what is going to happens. Gives out role cards.	
Decide on exactly *who* you are. Think of your lifestyle.	Asks them to consider their roles.	Think about their attitudes.
First of all, write down what life is like at the moment as if you are writing a short note to a friend who is living abroad. Then write what you think it will be like when the bridge has been built.	Gives writing task. Gives time for thoughts to be written down.	Write in role. Repeat, but thinking of the new situation.
Compare notes in your groups.	Encourages interaction.	Work in their groups.
You want to prepare for the meeting. What points do you wish to make? Have you any background knowledge that will add to your argument? Take time to research and gather any evidence you may wish to present to the public meeting. The people of Inverbrae may collaborate – as may the people of Scaravoe.	Directs as to how they *may* wish to proceed, making sure they work in role.	Interact, negotiate, collaborate, research, provide knowledge, while remaining in role. Members of groups may wish to communicate with other groups.

The Sea

Note:
*This letter should be
photocopied for use
in the lesson*

To the Chairman of the Public Enquiry
Inverbrae Public Hall

Dear Sir or Madam,

I thought you should know as soon as possible that the divers
working for the firm investigating suitable sites for the bridge
foundations have made some interesting discoveries.
Early this morning, a diver spotted something unusual. After
scraping the barnacles off, he realised it was the barrel of a
gun! Other objects could be seen lying close by, and on
bringing one to the surface, it seems to be a golden jug, of
Spanish style from the 16th century.
This discovery will mean that work must be stopped until it is
decided how we shall proceed, and I am making sure that no
unauthorised diving will take place.

Yours faithfully

James Buchanan,
Chief Inspector of Police

Lesson title

The Bridge Question (2)

Levels: **D/E** Key Stages **2/3** Levels **5–7**	OUTCOME/ ATTAINMENT TARGET	STRANDS
Date:	**Using** materials, techniques, skills and media	Investigating and experimenting: **a) investigate the immediate problem of 'the bridge'** **b) look at suitable ways in which to deal with the introduction of 'the wreck'** Using movement and mime: **show understanding of how their character would react** Using language: **a) use appropriately** **b) contribute to future planning**
Learning Aims: 1 **Research a topic** 2 **Develop a role and understand the attitudes and opinions experienced** 3 **Explore and develop the issues that arise using different drama strategies**		
Resources: **Role cards (supplied)** **Paper for writing task** **Letter from the Chief Inspector**	**Expressing** feelings,ideas, thoughts and solutions	Creating and designing: **collaborate in working towards the problem facing the villagers and the islanders** Communicating and presenting: **a) communicate effectively** **b) collaborate in organising future work**
Organisation: Session Two – **Public Enquiry** 1 **Interruption** 2 **Planning for future activities**	**Evaluating** and **Appreciating**	Observing, listening, reflecting, describing and responding: **reflect on what has been learned from the experience of the enquiry; comment on the contributions; respond to the situation by deciding on suitable future work**

Lesson Outline	Teacher Role	Pupil Activity
Second Session: The Public Enquiry		
When I re-enter the room, I shall be the Civil Servant from Edinburgh, who has come to listen to the people whose lives will be affected by the proposed bridge.	Sets the context.	
	Sets up the room as the public hall where the meeting is taking place. (Make sure you have everything you might need.)	Help to organise the space. Prepare to go into role.
	Makes sure the groups are in place, and in role.	Take up roles and relevant positions in the room.
	Exits, then enters in role.	
Good morning, ladies and gentlemen. I am —, and I'm here to listen to all the points being presented. It is my duty to take all the views which have been expressed to St Andrew's House in Edinburgh.	Establishes the discipline of the meeting.	
Before I begin the meeting, can I have all the names of the persons who wish to make a statement?	Asks for commitment from participants. Lists names.	Volunteer to speak publicly.
After all the statements have been heard, the meeting will then be open for debate.	Outlines future activity.	
Statements are heard – no interruptions are allowed.	Controls the meeting.	Make statements, listen and make notes.
The meeting is now open for debate. I may interrupt to ask for further background information.	Asks for others now to offer their opinions.	Contribute in response to what has previously been said.
Open-ended	Controls in role.	
	Allows time for the debate.	
Excuse me, I have just received a message that there is some urgent information for all those present.	Introduces the *tension* of the unknown.	
	Exits. Returns with letter. Reads it silently. Pauses.	
Ladies and gentlemen, as you know, preliminary diving is		

Lesson Outline	Teacher Role	Pupil Activity
being carried out to determine the best position for the bridge piles.		
A few hours ago, a diver spotted something unusual. He saw a strange long object. On scraping the barnacles off, he realised it was the barrel of a gun. On closer inspection, other objects could be seen. He brought a small item to the surface. After examination it appears to be a jug, made of gold. It looks like the type of flagon made in Spain during the 16th century. Now this changes everything!	Changes the focus of the lesson.	Listen to the new evidence.
Freeze!	Comes out of role, and brings the class out of role.	Respond to teacher.
Why has everything changed?	Queries.	Do they realise the importance of the discovery?
Discussion	Leads discussion.	Offer opinions.
Now our drama can go in several ways. (Only if you wish the class to choose *their* way of continuing the drama!)	Offers drama options *or* decides on future activity, depending on the needs of the class.	
Suggested Options		
We could go back into the past and pursue the history of the sunken vessel. We could be treasure seekers. What happens now to Inverbrae and Scaravoe? Could we tie up some of these ideas into a TV programme (see the suggestions below)?	With the class, plan for future drama activities.	Either decide on the path they wish to follow, or, under direction, start to plan ahead.

Suggestions for TV Programme

The environment of the village and the island could be considered, including the new interested parties who will have different priorities.
The story of the sunken vessel could be retold, using mixed media, and/or dance/drama.
Are there descendents of the shipwrecked sailors living in the area? (Current research in blood-sampling in Orkney hopes to prove people of Spanish descent are living there.)
Pupils can research suitable music, props and costume.
Not all may want to be performers. Student directors, floor managers and so on can experience the work and effort that goes into the production of a programme.

FROM CLASSROOM TO STAGE

(Three Drama Sessions plus Ideas for an Integrated Arts Project)

Introduction A drama session begins this topic, and, if you wish, the second and third could follow immediately, thereby just concentrating on the enactment of the legend, but this story lends itself to exploration in many other areas, and suggestions are given that demonstrate possibilities for a wider interpretation.

If the involvement of the pupils is intense, they will wish to share the results of their achievement with others, and this topic shows how everyday classroom work can be turned into a 'show piece' presentation without too much further effort.

Lesson title

Perseus and the Gorgon's Head

	OUTCOME/ ATTAINMENT TARGET	STRANDS
Levels: C/D **Key Stage 2** **Levels 3–5** Date: Learning Aims: 1 **Experience and experiment with a Greek myth** 2 **Integrate other expressive arts areas within the topic** 3 **Make decisions and solve problems**	**Using** materials, techniques, skills and media	Investigating and experimenting: **experimenting with movement, speech, space and sound, showing imagination and inventiveness** Using movement and mime: **using gesture and movement appropriate to role** Using language: **using language and sound appropriate to adopted roles**
Resources: **The story; soft balls (see p. 98)** **Musical instruments** **Materials for masks, costumes etc**	**Expressing** feelings, ideas, thoughts and solutions	Creating and designing: **develop roles, discuss and work on drama tasks and suggest solutions as to the creation of a performance** Communicating and presenting: **work co-operatively with others and participate in small-scale presentations**
Organisation 1 **The lessons should take place at first in the classroom, with desks pushed aside to allow some space for moving** 2 **When the class feels it is ready, a move to a room with more space is advisable** 3 **The teacher acts as story teller and supports the group work as the participants experiment with the different characters** 4 **As the pupils become more confident, they are encouraged to solve problems using a cross-curricular approach** 5 **The pupils should have the final decision as to whether their work is worthy of public presentation**	**Evaluating** and **Appreciating**	Observing, listening, reflecting, describing and responding: **participate in positive discussion and express opinions on the drama activities**

First Drama Session:
Perseus Starts his Journey

Perseus was a Greek prince. His mother was married to King Polydectes, and the King hated Perseus because his Mother doted on him so much! Now, Perseus was a bold young lad, and very adventurous. One day Polydectes thought up a plan to get Perseus to leave the court.

'Are you looking for something really exciting to do?' he asked Perseus slyly.

'Of course I am!' cried Perseus.

'Then what about cutting off the head of the Medusa. If you do that, you'll be extremely famous!'

He knew that Perseus could not resist such a challenge, but he also knew something Perseus did *not* know, and that was that the Medusa was one of three Gorgons, and she was the only one that could be slain.

The Gorgons were winged monsters, with teeth like the tusks of a wild boar, hands of brass and snakes instead of hair. No one seemed to know where they lived. Sailors who found their island by chance never returned home.

However, Perseus set off, but although he asked everyone he met, he could not find anyone who could tell him where their island was.

One day he met a young man who wore winged sandals and a winged cap, carrying a wand with two golden serpents twined round it. Now the Greeks, especially princes, were used to meeting their Gods face to face, so Perseus was not surprised, but pleased, because he knew that this was the God Hermes, and he could probably help him.

And indeed, Hermes said, 'Well done, Perseus. It is time someone got rid of the Medusa, but you'll need certain things to help you. You'll need winged sandals, just like mine, the magic bag that adjusts to fit what is inside it and the helmet of invisibility. These things are owned by the Nymphs of the North. I am not allowed to tell you where *they* live, but I can take you to the old Grey Women. They'll be able to tell you, but I warn you, they do not give up their secrets easily.

'They have to share *one* eye between the three of them. Snatch it from them as they pass it from one to another, and do not give it back until you hear what you want to hear.

'Now take my special sword. You'll need it, as no ordinary sword can hack through the Medusa's scales!'

'Thanks,' said Perseus. 'Let's go!'

'Wait!' a voice called out: and it was the Goddess Athene.

'Hermes, you have not told Perseus the greatest danger of all. Any man who looks at the Gorgons is turned into stone. What use is your sword?

'Take my silver shield, Perseus! Walk backwards as you approach the monsters and look at their reflections in the shield.'

And with these instructions, she disappeared into the clouds.

Hermes took Perseus on a long journey, until they reached the ends of the earth – and there were the three old Grey Women, arguing amongst themselves as they always did, as each wanted to have the one eye for as long as possible...

Lesson Outline	Teacher Role	Pupil Activity
Introduction		
Read/tell the first part of the story.	Story teller.	Listen.
Development		
Divide into groups of four: ie Perseus; and three Old Grey Women.	Organises. Allocates roles, if necessary. Gives a soft ball (representing the eye) to each group.	Adopt roles.
When I say 'Go!', the Old Grey Women start arguing, and toss the one eye from one to another... Perseus, try and catch it! Go!	Directs.	Listen to directions.
	Monitors the action.	Act out, using the ball as the eye.
Freeze.		
Well, Perseus, have you caught the eye?	Queries.	Respond.
If not, (which is highly likely!): Old Grey Women, throw it again, and this time, let him catch it, or we'll never hear the end of the story!	With humour, encourages group co-operation.	Co-operate in acting-out.
Freeze, and sit down.	Controls.	Respond to control.
Now listen carefully: those who are the Old Grey Women in your groups must decide where the Nymphs of the North live. It is quite a complicated journey. Perseus, you can listen, but you must not speak and make any suggestions! You will have to repeat everything they say to you, when we start the story again.	Asks them to make their own decisions.	Concentrate, negotiate and listen.
You have *two minutes* to make up the journey.	Give *tension* of time. (Allow no longer!)	Have to work quickly to complete the task.
Freeze! Do you all know the details of the journey?	Controls and monitors progress.	Demonstrate commitment to task.
Perseus, give the eye to one of the Old Grey Women.	Directs.	

Lesson Outline	Teacher Role	Pupil Activity
Now listen again, carefully. When I say 'Go!', Women – throw the eye between you three times, letting Perseus catch it on the third throw. When he catches the eye, what will you say to him?	Outlines the forthcoming action. (Why has he stolen the eye? Have they got information to give him?)	Listen. Do they fully understand the story, and what they have planned?
Perseus, you will only give back the eye when you can repeat the precise details of the journey.	Directs Perseus.	
Are you ready? Take up starting positions. Go!	Waits until there is silence. (Remember the drama can be stopped at any time. You are asking them to remember quite a complicated scene, and they will need support.)	Prepare.
Freeze!	Controls.	Respond.
Try the scene again!	Gives opportunity for them to improve their work.	They may wish to discuss before repeating.
Which group would like to show what it has worked out?	Asks for volunteers.	(Some may be more confident than others.)
Do not begin until everyone is sitting quietly, ready to watch!	Introduces 'audience awareness and responsibility'.	Group holds starting position.
Go!	Watches and comments on the parts where they have been successful. Only if they are being 'silly' and have obviously not tried, do you stop them, and suggest that they need to think more carefully.	Group(s) present their work.
Reflection and Evaluation		
Discuss positively the work presented.	Leads discussion.	Evaluate their own and others' work.
Moving on		
Now the next part of the story deals with the Nymphs of the North, who are very happy people.	Asks the pupils to think ahead.	Listen.
This is a fantasy story. How do you think we could represent the Nymphs?	Asks for advice.	Look for solutions.

Lesson Outline	Teacher Role	Pupil Activity
And looking further into the future, we'll also need to think about the Gorgons: for example, how they might move; as well as how we might present them.	Asks them to think technically.	Consider.
Could we compose Gorgon music? Let's think about all this...	Asks the class to relate the drama experiences to other Expressive Arts areas. (I suggest here that you leave the drama until you and the class have worked on other areas related to the topic. See suggestions for following sessions.)	Widen their perspectives.

Suggestions for Following Sessions

After the first Drama Session, which is the introduction to the Expressive Arts topic, other elements can be introduced. It will depend on your own ideas on managing and organising a topic as to how this might be done.

In Art and Design, for example, the pupils could decide on how the Nymphs in the legend might be represented. Would they wish to use puppets or work with masks? The Gorgons' masks will also need to be designed, as might simple representational costume. You might wish to wait until the pupils have their first ideas for masks available before you ask them to invent 'sound pictures' or 'signature tunes' for the characters, which will convey the mood and atmosphere? The children and you can decide whether the music will inspire the movements of the characters, or the strange creatures' actions and gestures will dictate the rhythms of the musical inventions.

The preparation for the enactment of the whole story should flow easily from one medium to another, until the children are satisfied with what they are producing, and whether they wish to share this with a wider audience.

OUTCOMES AND STRANDS
The other Expressive Arts areas feature in this series. Therefore attainment targets can be sought over a wide range of activities. However, you should not attempt to record specifically on every task the pupils undertake. Decisions must be reached as to what you are looking for. Assessment need not, and some would say, should not occur within every session. I have made a brief list of the areas in the Expressive Arts that could be assessed if it is thought desirable, but this topic has potential for exciting language tasks, and could easily provide the basis for work that provides evidence of attainment using a cross-curricular approach.

ART AND DESIGN	*Using a range of material, make masks or puppets*
	Discuss problems in design and attempt to solve them
MUSIC	*Experiment with different combinations and qualities of sound*
	Use a range of instruments, demonstrating contrasts
PHYSICAL EDUCATION	*Work co-operatively with others, presenting own compositions*
	Link actions together and refine movement skills
	Apply skills with control
	Show work and offer evaluative comment

Lesson Outline	Teacher Role	Pupil Activity
Second Drama Section: Perseus Meets the Gorgon		
Introduction		
We shall continue in our acting out of the story, and today we will discover what happened to Perseus.	Outlines the context.	Prepare to work.
	(If puppets and/or masks have been made for the Nymphs of the North, use them for a *short* improvisation as described below. If not, then remind the pupils of the objects Perseus obtained from them and continue at 'Development' below.)	
Using the masks or puppets that have been made, Perseus approaches the Nymphs of the North and explains what he wishes to do. The Nymphs hand over the sandals, the bag and the helmet.	Directs acting out in groups.	Act out using their own contributions to the drama.
Development		
Into groups of four.	Prepares for the new context.	Prepare to continue the story.
Perseus and three Gorgons.	Organises the roles.	Adopt roles.
The Gorgons are lying asleep.	Directs.	Take up positions.
I shall be Athene: 'Listen carefully, Perseus, to what I will say to you....	TIR as Athene.	Prepare to work with TIR.
Put on the helmet ... Now you are invisible ... Hold up the shield ... *Do not look at the Gorgons!* Move backwards towards them... *Stop!* The Medusa is the one nearest you... *Cut off her head* Put it in the bag. *Well done!*	Directs in role as Athene, slowing down the action and building up the tension.	Perseus listens to Athene, and and obeys her instructions.
Freeze.	Controls the action.	Hold a tableau position.
Remaining Gorgons: what will you do?	Out of role, questions.	Respond appropriately.

Lesson Outline	Teacher Role	Pupil Activity
Perseus, what do you have on that will allow you to escape? *Go!*	Monitors the chase.	Act out.
Freeze.		
Repeat this section from the beginning. I will be Athene helping you.	Allows them to consolidate the action.	Repeat the scene.
Now into groups of five: Perseus; three Gorgons; and Athene this time.	Reorganises groups.	Change groups.
You have *two* minutes to prepare your own version of the scene we have just done.	Gives *tension* of time.	Prepare fairly quickly.
Do you want any music?	Makes them think of atmosphere. Moves around the groups, helping only if necessary.	Plan and consider ways of building atmosphere.
All start your scenes *now*.	Controls and monitors.	Groups work simultaneously.
Freeze!		
Does any group wish to show its work?	Gives opportunity for presenting.	Volunteer if they wish.

Reflection and Evaluation

Positive discussion on work presented.	Leads discussion.	Reflect and evaluate.

The Story Ends

To be read at the beginning of Session Three.

Now Perseus had the Gorgon's head so he set off towards home.
The court was waiting for him, and King Polydectes laughed: 'I see no sign of the Gorgon's head, Perseus. Away all this time – and no results?'
'I shall prove to you I killed the Medusa! All of those of you who are my friends – hide your eyes!'
And from the bag he brought forth the head – making sure he did not look at it himself.
Immediately the King and *his* friends were turned to stone.
'Put the head in the bag and give it to me!' The voice was that of Athene. 'And I shall take your sandals and your helmet. You are only a human being – not a God!'
So Perseus gave up the magic objects, and took his Mother away from the court of stone.

Lesson Outline	Teacher Role	Pupil Activity
Third Drama Session: *(not counting reinforcement sessions that may have taken place!)* **Perseus Returns**		
Introduction		
Read/tell the end of the story.	Story teller.	Listen.
Shall we act out the last part of the story?	Queries.	Hopefully, by this time, the class will be expecting to do just that!
Divide the children into two groups, each including Perseus, Polydectes, Athene, Courtiers and Mother.	Organises groups and space.	Prepare to work.
Groups are left to work out the action – adding sound effects and music as they wish.	Watches – helps, if asked.	Not every child might adopt a role: Stage management might interest some.
Groups volunteer to present their work.	Helps with organisation.	Watch, and present.
Evaluate.	Leads evaluation.	Give honest criticism.
Reflection and Discussion		
Having acted out this story, could we put it all together and add parts to make a Greek play?	(Only if you feel it is suitable do you suggest this. The process of building up to this session may be enough.)	
If they agree, discuss what is needed to turn it into a presentation for an audience.		Consider the implications of presenting the story before an audience.
How will they cast it? Who will be in charge of props? Who will play the music? What needs to be added? What needs to be worked upon and improved?	(Suggestion: a Greek Chorus can help tell the story.)	Make decisions.

Perseus and the Gorgon's Head: **SUGGESTED CAST LIST**	STAGE MANAGEMENT TEAM *(If masks are used, all characters, except Perseus, can also play other roles)* PERSEUS KING POLYDECTES HERMES ATHENE	PERSEUS' MOTHER THE THREE OLD GREY WOMEN THE THREE NYMPHS OF THE NORTH THE THREE GORGONS GREEK CHORUS *(who provide the story links)* MUSICIANS COURTIERS

Assessment and Recording

Assessment Every school will have its own assessment policy, and what follows is advice on how to begin assessing the drama work of your class.

Do not try to assess every child during every drama session, and indeed you should think of assessing only when it is appropriate. Each lesson here is preceded by a list of the Attainment Targets and Strands, so when you wish to assess, guidance is given as to *what* you should be looking for.

Keep a note of the time taken to accomplish tasks and look out for those who are having difficulties with the tasks that have been set: they will probably not have reached that level. It does not mean that these children are not 'good' at drama, but that they need more practice and confidence in certain areas. For example, a child might be extremely able at planning and organising a group prior to acting out, but may become tongue-tied when involved in the presentation. He or she needs more experience in simple exercises in acting out, without the pressure of showing the work to others (see Recording). Older pupils could keep a 'drama diary'. This can provide the basis for the pupil to be involved in his or her own self-assessment of their progress and performance.

Peer assessment in drama needs to be handled carefully. You will need to stress to the class that *positive* evaluation is more helpful and encouraging than merely stating what could be improved.

Check that you are including a variety of styles of drama lessons, which means that all strands are being covered.

Recording In your usual forward plan/record of work, note the drama lesson and the level that is being attained. *There* and *then*, note the children for whom you will need to adjust the content of future lessons. An example is given below.

12/01/94 Drama **Resistance Workers** Level D
Next steps NB all children need practice in miming skills/Level C.

8/03/94 Drama **The Sad Giant** Level B
All now concentrating.
Working well at Level B.

17/06/94 Drama **Perseus** Level C
Class working at Level C.
NB John Smith at Level D for planning and organising *but* Level B in presentation skills.
Next steps Whole class would benefit from more teacher-led group work, slowing down the action and demonstrating care in sharing small group work with others.

Bibliography

Katie Morag and the Two Grandmothers

M. Hedderwick, *Katie Morag and the Two Grandmothers*, Bodley Head, 1986

The Six Lives of Fankle the Cat

T. Allan, *The Time Traveller Book of Pharaohs and Pyramids*, Usborne, 1977

G. Mackay Brown, *The Six Lives of Fankle the Cat*, Canongate, 1984

T.G.H. James, *Pharaoh's People: Scenes from Life in Imperial Egypt*, Bodley Head, 1984

J. Vercoutter, *The Search for Ancient Egypt*, (New Horizon series), Thames and Hudson, 1992

Flannan Isle

The Scots Magazine, D.C. Thomson, September 1984

F. Thompson, *Victorian and Edwardian Highlands from Old Photographs*, Tantallon Books, 1989

Yachting Monthly, IPC Magazines, October 1990

The Desperate Journey

K. Fidler, *The Desperate Journey*, Canongate, 1985

Children in War

A. Frank, *The Diary of Anne Frank*, Pan Horizons, 1989

Scottish Memories, Memories Magazine, October 1993

B. Wicks, *The Day they took the Children*, ISIS, 1990

Perseus and the Gorgon's Head

C. Evans and A. Millard, *Greek Myths and Legends*, Usborne, 1985

R. Gibson, *The Usborne Book of Masks*, Usborne, 1993

More Ideas for Drama

A. Brittin, *Starting Points for Drama*, Arnold-Wheaton, 1987

N. McCaslin, *Creative Drama in the Classroom*, Longman, 1990

C. O'Neil and A. Lambert, *Drama Structures: A Practical Handbook for Teachers*, Hutchinson, 1984

C. O'Neil et al, *Drama Guidelines*, Heinemann, 1977

G. Rawlings and J. Rich, *Look, Listen and Trust: A Framework for Learning through Drama*, Macmillan, 1992

A.Scher, *Another 100+ Ideas for Drama*, Heinemann, 1987

S. Smith, *The Primary Drama Handbook*, Ward Lock Educational, 1983

Suggestions for Background Reading

G.Davies, *Practical Primary Drama*, Heinemann, 1983

C. Evary and L. Smith, *Acting and Theatre*, Usborne, 1992

L. McGregor et al, *Learning through Drama: Schools Council Drama Teaching Project*, Heinemann, 1977

J. Neelands, *Making Sense of Drama: A Guide to Classroom Practice*, Heinemann, 1985

B. Woolland, *The Teaching of Drama in the Primary School*, Longman, 1994

Scotland

Curriculum and Assessment in Scotland National Guidelines: Expressive Arts 5–14, (SOED) HMSO, 1992

Some Aspects of Thematic Work, (COPE), HMSO, 1987

England and Wales

Aspects of Primary Education: The Teaching and Learning of Drama, (DES) HMSO, 1990

English in the National Curriculum (DFE) HMSO, 1995